PRAISE FOR
A Marriage of Equals

"ThirdPath Institute works with couples who aspire to create *A Marriage of Equals*. This book will now become the resource I strongly recommend to help them achieve their goals. In a world with very little guidance, and lots of obstacles, Catherine Aponte provides straightforward advice to help couples stay on track to creating healthy and happy relationships. First describing the beauty and strength of collaborative negotiation, then explaining how conflict often escalates to self-protective strategies that derail creative problem solving, *A Marriage of Equals* then outlines a number of antidotes to avoid this problem. Thank you, Dr. Aponte for creating such an important resource for couples who are looking for a new and better way to live happily every after."

—Jessica DeGroot, Founder and President,
The Third Path Institute (www.thirdpath.org)

"What a pleasure to find such an insightful, helpful, and realistic discussion of what it means to have an equal marriage and what it takes to create one. If you are seeking an egalitarian partnership and a set of concrete strategies to achieve it, this is the book to read."

—Kathleen Gerson, Ph.D.,
Professor of Sociology and Collegiate Professor of Arts and Science at New York University, and author of
An Unfinished Revolution: How a New Gen~~~~~~ Is Reshaping Fam~~~~~~~~~~~~~~~~~~~~~~~~~~~~~a

"*A Marriage of Equals* does what no other book available does—speak to today's heterosexual couples who want to have an egalitarian marriage. In clear and respectful language, Catherine Aponte walks men and women through having thoughtful conversations that address gendered expectations and stereotypes that still plague couples no matter how much they want to live differently, and gives them the tools to make that happen."
—Vicki Larson, award-winning journalist and co-author of
The New I Do: Reshaping Marriage for Skeptics,
Realists and Rebels

"Dr. Aponte's 'collaborative negotiation' approach has the potential to really shift dialogues and dynamics in couples just beginning their partnerships, as well as help 'seasoned' couples who are stuck in conflict. The book is a challenge to all of us to not let societally proscribed gender roles dictate our expectations of ourselves and our partners in marriage. In short, this book answers the question about how to create a more equitable, just society related to gender. Her work gives me hope that such societal change is possible. She has certainly impacted how I think about and engage in marriage, and I trust everyone who reads her book will be impacted as well. I would recommend the book to couples considering marriage, those wishing to enhance their marriage, as well as to therapists who work with couples in distress and academicians who are teaching the next generation of therapists how to do couples work."
—Brenda Futrell Nash, Ph.D. Director of Clinical Training,
School of Professional Psychology, Spalding University,
Louisville, KY

"Based on decades of clinical practice and supervision, [Aponte] has written a wise book that is theoretically sound (neo-cognitive and interpersonal), with fresh insights on sex and monogamy. As a practicing psychologist who specializes in couples, I will enthusiastically recommend this accessible, compelling and relevant book to any couple—especially young couples!"

—Scott Salathe, Psy.D., Salathe Behavior Health, Individual and Couples Therapy, Clinical Faculty School of Professional Psychology, Spalding University, Louisville, KY

"I loved the Takeaways at the end of each chapter and wish every self help style book did this. You discuss many different points that can strengthen a marriage. I liked the idea of collaborative negotiation and how positively it can impact all marriages. Couples do need to recognize that to flourish as a couple, they need to flourish as individuals. This book made me realize how critical self-reflection is, the importance of identifying insecurities and working through them, and how we need to understand each other's concerns."

—Greg W., Construction Company Project Manager, lives in Louisville, Kentucky

A

MARRIAGE

of

EQUALS

A

MARRIAGE

of

EQUALS

HOW TO ACHIEVE BALANCE IN A
COMMITTED RELATIONSHIP

CATHERINE E. APONTE, PSY.D.

Clinical Psychologist

SHE WRITES PRESS

Published 2019

Printed in the United States of America
ISBN: 978-1-63152-497-4 pbk
ISBN: 978-1-63152-498-1 ebk
Library of Congress Control Number: 2018962995

For information, address:
She Writes Press
1569 Solano Ave #546
Berkeley, CA 94707

She Writes Press is a division of SparkPoint Studio, LLC.

Book design by Stacey Aaronson

CONTENTS

PART V: HOW THE REVOLUTION CAN STALL

FOREWORD

It is with pleasure that I write the foreword for *A Marriage of Equals: How to Achieve Balance in a Committed Relationship*. This book is the by-product of Dr. Catherine E. Aponte's extensive professional career and personal life experiences. The book reflects Catherine's academic education and training, her teaching and supervision of doctoral-level psychology students, her experiences working with couples in her private clinical practice, and her real-life experiences in a long-term marriage. All these experiences are pulled together from a psychological perspective in a cogent, well-organized, and comprehensive manner that will set you on a path to looking at yourself, your partner, and your relationship.

The concepts, principles, and concrete steps identified by Catherine in this book are grounded in solid psychological and sociological research. Part I ("The Revolution at Home") and Part II ("The Personal Revolution") lay the foundation for what follows in the remaining chapters of the book. Parts III ("The Revolution in the Bedroom") and Part IV ("The Revolution at Work") delve into the practical application of the concepts and principals, and step into the arenas of sex, family and work, and parenting. Part V ("How the Revolution Can Stall") addresses ways in which this approach to marriage can be undermined—i.e., gender traps. In addition, managing difficult situations, such as when your partner is mentally ill, is addressed in this part of the book.

Collaborative negotiation, according to Catherine, is a critical element in achieving your equitable marriage. This concept in not the structured and staid version of negotiation presented by business or psychotherapeutic literature and practice. Rather, Catherine describes a dynamic process that defines *collaborative negotiation* in Chapter 1. Simultaneously seeing oneself as an individual and seeing yourself as a couple is an important part of this process. In order for *collaborative negotiation* to work, each person in the relationship must be self-reflective and value their partner.

Several of the concepts discussed by Catherine in Parts I and II of this book enrich our appreciation and understanding of marital dynamics and are crucial for *collaborative negotiation*. Simple but important concepts, such as *needs vs. wants* and *disagreements vs. conflicts*, are described in Chapters 1 and 2, respectively. Catherine articulates how understanding these concepts will allow us to better understand ourselves and the interpersonal interactions that are central to marital relationships. Another important concept is *taking things personally*, which is discussed in Chapter 3 of the book. Taking things personally reflects the self-protective strategies we all use (which are discussed in Chapter 4). These self-protective strategies are formed, as many psychologists argue, by our early childhood experiences.

Although this is not a how-to book, there are a number of practical steps and exercises both in the body of the book and in the appendices. For example, in Chapter 1, Catherine lays out four concrete steps in the negotiation process, from approaching your partner to making a win-win action plan. In Chapter 3, a series of steps is laid out to address your personal insecurities that may have a negative impact on your relationship with your spouse. Taking a personal inventory and reflecting on the sources of these insecurities is a critical part of addressing them. Appendix C, the "Taking Things Personally Worksheet," provides a detailed and systematic guide to learn more about yourself and engage in more constructive interactions with your spouse.

At a personal level, Catherine and I have used many of the concepts, principles, and steps in our relationship throughout our marriage. From complicated career choices to simple decisions such as going to the movies, practicing self-reflection, identifying personal preferences, and engaging in collaborative negotiation are the cornerstones of our relationship. In these situations, when friction occurs between us, it is likely a result of one of us taking things personally. When this occurs, it is difficult to agree on how to move forward on such decisions. This is a signal to each of us to be self-reflective and look at each of our parts in our interactions. Using this process requires hard work, but applying it to our marriage has made our relationship stronger.

A Marriage of Equals will challenge you to look differently at yourself, your partner, and the relationship you share. Although this book focuses on young men and women interested in creating and sustaining an equitable marriage, the concepts, principles, and steps described in the pages that follow have application to all age groups and several different types of relationships. The book may be the capstone of Catherine's professional career, but it certainly is not the capstone of our marriage. We continuously look at ourselves, value the other, and collaboratively negotiate our differences. Through this process, we will continue to sustain and enhance our marital relationship well into the future.

—Joseph F. Aponte, PhD
Emeritus Professor of Psychology
Department of Psychological and Brain Sciences
University of Louisville

PREFACE

I am a clinical psychologist who is married to a clinical psychologist, Joseph F. Aponte. We married in 1960, a time of significant social change. Joe had his PhD and I had a BS when we moved to Chapel Hill, NC, in 1970, where Joe took his first job. We had been married ten years, and I had decided I wanted to go to graduate school for a degree in psychology. This created a problem for us, since he had already earned his degree and was ready to begin his career in psychology. Of course, by this time, his status and earning power were higher than mine (and would forever remain so). What this meant to me—and to most other women in this situation—was that what I wanted to do was limited to some degree by my husband's greater earning power and by a late start on my career.

Until this time of social upheaval in the perception of and status of women, I had not considered seeking a doctorate. It just was not on the radar for most women at that time. In addition, no one in my lower-middle-class family had ever graduated from college. Because of the changing status of women during the 1960s and 1970s, however, I was now aware that I had options I had not previously thought I had.

When I decided that I wanted to earn a doctor of psychology degree, Joe, to his great credit, "got it." And so we embarked upon a marital journey guided by the basic principle that neither one of our careers was more important than the other's. Ultimately, I did earn my doctoral degree in psychology, and in the ensuing years I built a successful private practice working primarily with couples. Joe, meanwhile, took an academic route.

This book is based on my own lived experience during the feminist revolution of the '70s with my loving and supportive husband, through my excellent training as a psychologist at the University of Florida, Duke University, and Spalding University, and finally as a practicing psychologist who worked with couples for over thirty years.

Most of the couples I saw over the years sought counseling only after experiencing significant difficulties in their relationship for a long time. Many had traditional marriages. Even if the women worked, they carried either the responsibility for and/or guilt about caring for their children. Both partners had become bitter, angry, demoralized, and resistant to looking at their individual part in the relationship's problems.

In my work with couples, I always emphasized the notion that the capacity for self-awareness through self-reflection is fundamental to being in an intimate relationship with another person. As noted, many of the couples with whom I worked have had rather traditional gender relationships. Once entrenched, gender patterns in a marriage are not easily changed. Women who had been stay-at-home mothers for years were not easily going to embark upon a career. Husbands used to wives who catered to them did not readily seek help. Once you go down a traditional, gendered path, it is virtually impossible to create or re-create an egalitarian relationship.

I am writing this book for young couples who are beginning their marriages with an historically unprecedented belief: there are no inherently male or female prescribed roles for being good husbands and wives. The jury is still out on the question of whether these young couples will be able to sustain this commitment to gender equality in marriage, of course.

Kathleen Gerson, a sociologist, interviewed young adults who grew up in the tumultuous post-feminist period that saw sea changes in family life: the transition to two-paycheck parents, and the rise of single parents, cohabiting, and same-sex marriage. Despite the entrance of women into the workforce and the blurring of once clearly defined gender boundaries, men and women today live in a world in which the demands of balancing parenting and work, autonomy and commitment, and time and money are left largely unresolved. Gerson's work, described in the aptly named *The Unfinished Revolution*, shows that an overwhelming majority of young men and women see an equitable balance within committed relationships as the ideal. However, because the majority of the world's social and economic realities remain based on traditional (and now obsolete) distinctions between breadwinning and caretaking, many of these young men and women seem to be falling short of their desired outcomes in their relationships—reverting to traditional approaches, for example, or avoiding marriage completely.

My goal in this book is to help you start your own revolution by turning your relationship into a committed and equitable marriage. By doing this, you will not only benefit yourself, you'll benefit your society. The perspective I take is psychological rather than sociological—that is, I will focus in the chapters to come on how the dynamics between you and your spouse can help or hinder the achievement of both a committed and egalitarian marriage.

Cocreating a committed and equitable marriage is vital because: 1) women today are more likely to abstain from marriage altogether than to live in a traditional marriage; 2) good relationships in the context of marriage are good both for us as individuals and for our greater society; 3) having both mother and father equally invested (equal joy and equal sacrifice) in raising their children is good for everyone; and 4) women will not achieve equality in society as a whole if they live in a gender-defined relationship.

I want to share with you what I have gained from my path to a committed and equitable marriage. I hope you'll join me on this journey.

INTRODUCTION

You are living in a time when the demands of balancing parenting and work, autonomy and commitment, and time and money have been left largely unresolved. While most of you want an equitable and committed marriage, social and economic pressures continue to work against you.

Most of what is written about having an equitable marriage takes a sociological perspective on how to change the workplace and social attitudes, and to provide social support. My approach to finishing the revolution, however, is a psychological one: I focus on the dynamics of an equitable marriage relationship. I promote marriages based on the willingness and ability of both husband and wife to organize their relationship around **collaboratively negotiating** with one another instead of living according to traditionally prescribed gender roles.

I have found that much advice about marriage is stuck in a traditional, gender-driven view of how things should work. Such approaches do nothing to change the outmoded model of marriage that I seek to disrupt. My approach is about fundamentally changing the way you think about being married so that you and your partner can create a better life for yourselves—and help change our society in the process.

Taking off on Kathleen Gerson's notion of an equitable

marriage being "an unfinished revolution," I have organized this book into the series of revolutions that must take place in order for you to create a new vision of marriage.[1] (You will find a summary of Gerson's study in Appendix A.) Part I describes the vision of creating an equitable marriage through collaborative negotiation around your individual and joint life plans. Here, I go into what it means to negotiate collaboratively (hint: it is not a zero-sum game). I also address ideas about needs vs. wants in marriage, as well as distinguish between having a disagreement or difference vs. being in conflict with one another. Next, I focus on the importance of learning to be self-reflective, which is about conscious consideration and analysis of your individual beliefs and actions.

Taking care of your personal issues is a fundamental element of creating and sustaining an equitable and satisfying marriage and maintaining your own personal well-being. Part II describes what this personal revolution is about. Understanding what it means when we say we "take something personally" is the place to start this revolution. When we are taking something personally, we are protecting our own self, our own ego. And when we do this, we're incapable of displaying the empathy and concern we must show in order to interact well, kindly, thoughtfully, and considerately with our spouse. Psychologists tell us that when we are taking things personally, we are experiencing a feeling of personal threat that is likely grounded in our childhood experiences. It is important to look at how such threatening feelings can occur and how they morph into adult self-protective strategies, which impede our ability to negotiate collaboratively with one another.

The next revolution I discuss in this book is the revolution in the bedroom. This revolution is about understanding the psychology of sex, not just following a how-to manual. This part of the book, Part III, is designed to help you co-construct your own sexual life rather than relying on old, stereotypical sexual scripts. To do so, you cannot get bogged down in old gender stereotypes about how men and women approach sex; you must become aware of your own old ideas about sex. It is important to understand that in marriage there is a tension between valuing the safety and security you get from a long-term relationship and the excitement of being separate and independent. The need for sexual adventure and excitement is hard to generate with the person you look to for comfort and stability. Generating excitement in marriage will create a certain amount of threat to the feeling of safety and security you get from being married. Negotiating your sexual preferences as you do all other issues in an equitable marriage, however, will lead to a satisfying and sustainable sexual relationship.

Throughout this book, I will advance the idea that to have an equitable marriage, you and your spouse must become increasingly self-reflective. As a husband, you can become more self-reflective about your sexual desire or libido, which can be a boon to your marital relationship. This section of the book is designed to stimulate your own thinking about your masculinity, how this relates to your sexual desire, and how this plays out in your marriage.

The issue of infidelity, or rather fidelity, in your marriage is part of your sexual revolution. You will want to be smart about what it means to make a commitment to sexual fidelity throughout your marriage. Even though we have an almost mythical belief in monogamy, society finds all kinds of ways to support or encourage infidelity. This attachment to the idea of monogamy may have its roots in our early experience of unconditional love given wholeheartedly by parents without our having to make any effort. Monogamy in a marriage, however, is not a given but a choice you and your spouse make together. Fidelity is a matter of conviction rather than convention.

We need a revolution in how to create time for family, work, community, and other life priorities. Part IV, therefore, focuses on the relationship between work and home and on shared parenting—balancing parenting and work, autonomy and commitment, and time and money. Managing household tasks, work, and child-rearing while caring for each other is not easy. Here, I give examples of couples who have figured out successful strategies for creating and maintaining balance in their lives.

Part V is about how your revolution can stall. There are real, intense social and economic pressures that get in the way of achieving an equitable marriage, and I address these issues bluntly here. For heterosexual couples, falling back on old ideas about gender roles in marriage will always be the "default" mode, particularly at times of transition in your lives. You must work to detach from the idea that how you act toward each other in your marriage defines your masculinity and femininity. Both of you must watch your resistance to the changes that must take place in order to establish and maintain an equitable relationship.

I focus primarily on heterosexual marriage in this book

because it is these marriages, rather than same-sex marriages, that are bound by the motif of gender that is incompatible with achieving an equitable relationship. In both my readings and my experience, I've found same-sex relationships are not dictated by a gender motif. While I do think that many of the ideas broached in this book are applicable to same-sex marriage, my overarching goal is to help heterosexual couples strive for and achieve an equitable marriage that is not organized around gender.

Creating an equitable marriage is an achievable goal. It takes a lot of effort, but it does work—and it's worth it!

PART I

THE REVOLUTION
AT HOME

1

A New Perspective

In order to achieve an equitable marriage, a husband and wife must maintain a simultaneous perspective of themselves both as individuals and as a couple; they must have a sense of "being in this together" while also having individual life plans. This kind of marriage is based on both partners' willingness and ability to negotiate the wants and desires that flow from their individual and joint life plans—plans that are not dictated by gender roles or gender traits. The schematic below shows the idea of having a simultaneous perspective in your marriage.

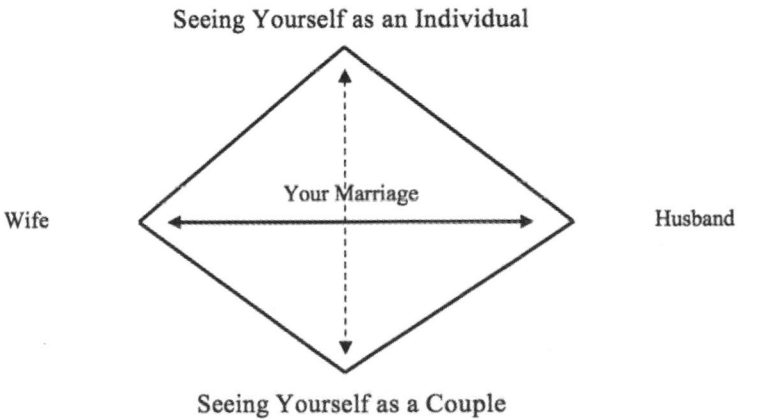

This schematic depicts the idea that husbands and wives can simultaneously see themselves as individuals in a marriage and see themselves as a couple. The horizontal line between wife and husband represents their marriage. The vertical dotted line represents the simultaneous perspective of being both an individual and a couple. If either person sees him/herself only or primarily as an individual, they will think primarily of her/himself in the marriage, precluding real negotiation. If either person sees him/herself only or primarily as being a couple, he/she will neglect his/her own wishes and wants, creating a codependent relationship.

Even though gender is becoming less significant in defining functions and relationships in most areas of our public lives, it remains a central motif in marriage. Sociologists believe this is the case because the idea of masculinity and femininity are acted out in marriage. Sociologist Sara Berk has described marriage as a "gender factory"—i.e., husbands and wives demonstrate their masculinity/femininity in the way they interact around everyday household activities, childcare, and displays of affection for one another.[1] Being masculine and feminine is our way of carrying out the roles of husband and wife. When we carry out these gender roles, we subconsciously assume it is because of innate gender differences in masculinity and femininity, which reinforces the idea that marriage should be organized by gender. An entirely new perspective is needed.

MARRIAGE AS COLLABORATIVE NEGOTIATION

———

The ongoing process of collaborative negotiation between self-reflective, equally valued partners is what sustains a marriage across time, over changing life situations, and through individual growth. The ongoing process of collaborative negotiation between self-reflective, equally valued partners is what maintains and enhances the feeling of love and mutual enjoyment with which most marital relationships begin. The ongoing process of collaborative negotiation between self-reflective, equally valued partners is what supports those partners' individual development in a marriage.

Negotiating collaboratively begins with both husband and wife being able to identify their own wants in any given situation. Once these wishes are stated, the next job is to provide reasons for them. It is as if each of you is putting these wishes on a virtual kitchen table, allowing agreement, differences, and disagreements to become apparent. From this perspective, differences and disagreements are on the table between you, not exclusively within either of you.

The schematic below depicts this idea: wants are openly stated, looked at side-by-side, and negotiated so that a win-win outcome can occur. The schematic also depicts clearly the idea that disagreements and/or differences are *between* the two of you, not within each of you.

Virtual Kitchen Table

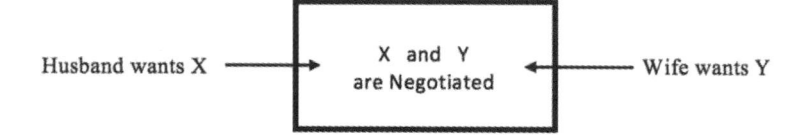

Husband wants X ⟶ | X and Y are Negotiated | ⟵ Wife wants Y

The negotiation that takes place in marriage is not the kind that one sees in business, where each party is trying to maximize his/her own gain at the expense of the other. Nor is it a quid pro quo (tit for tat, you do this for me and I will do that for you) kind of negotiation. Negotiating collaboratively has the following characteristics: 1) each partner understands that his/her spouse is as valuable a person as he/she is; 2) each partner is willing to negotiate his/her wants and desires; 3) each partner is able to identify wants and desires; 4) each partner can explain (not justify) what is important about their stated wants and desires; 5) neither partner seeks to "privilege" his or her wants and desires over the other's because of status (for example, gender or superior wage earning); 6) each partner is willing to take action based on the negotiation of wants and desires; 7) each partner is willing to accept the outcome of his/her individual actions taken; and 8) each partner is willing to learn and change based on the outcomes of actions taken.

The Myth of Reciprocity

Psychologist John Gottman argues against the idea that good marriages should be based on "reciprocity"—e.g., "You help me with vacuuming the house, and I'll help out by taking out the trash." This, he says, is often an unwritten agreement to offer something in return for each word or deed—and it's an approach to marriage that requires you to keep a running tally of who has done what for whom (how many times you vacuumed in exchange for your partner taking out the trash, in this case).

Gottman argues that this kind of unspoken contract is full of anger and resentment because each partner is consciously or subconsciously keeping score. Happy marriages are not about 50/50 transactions. In happy marriages, partners find a way to share tasks and feel good about their partner and their relationship.

The Seven Principles for Making Marriage Work by John Gottman, Crown Publishers, Inc., 1999.

NEEDS AND WANTS: IT'S NOT JUST SEMANTICS

———

To understand how the negotiation of wishes works, I must confront one of the most common ideas about how a marriage relationship should work—one that is the basis of many how-to marriage manuals and is promoted by many marriage counselors and therapists. This is the idea that marriage is about each of us fulfilling each other's *needs*.

In my work with couples, I have long stressed that when you are talking about the things in life that are important to you to live well, you should use the concept of "want" rather than the currently popular concept of "need." For example, saying to your spouse, "I want to have sex with you" is quite different than saying, "I need to have sex with you." While you might want to argue that this is semantics, it is not.

The concept of **need** became popular in psychology during the middle of the twentieth century as an expression of the more general idea that we are all motivated primarily (or only) by **self-interest**. This view is not new; in fact, it has been the dominant view in psychology and in much of Western thought in general for decades. When applied to intimate relationships, it translates into the idea that we must fulfill our partner's **self-identified individual needs**. (I say "self-identified" needs because there really is no way to identify a list of needs that is universally accepted.) Thus, in this view of things, we can call anything we want or prefer a need, without having to explain it.

Operating from this premise, almost all marriage advice has stuck with the idea that we must fulfill each other's needs —advice that can have toxic effects. These effects are:

+ Needs become demands that we feel entitled to have fulfilled.

+ Needs cannot be negotiated because they are entitlements; they are exchanged in tit-for-tat or quid-pro-quo arrangements (I'll have sex with you if you will spend more time talking to me).

+ Not to have a need fulfilled is an injustice that will breed resentment and justify bad behavior.

+ Partners value one another in terms of how well they fulfill their needs, implying that the other person has no intrinsic worth independent of how well they fulfill those needs.

+ There is no end to the list of things you can need. Any want, preference, or desire can be identified as a need.

+ You do not have to be concerned about how fulfilling your self-identified needs affects your partner, because you believe you are entitled to have them met.

+ People who promote this view tend to adopt the idea that men and women have biologically determined, inherent, and enduring different needs (e.g., men are from Mars and women are from Venus). In this view, husbands and wives must fulfill each other's biologically-based gender needs.

+ Not having your needs met is justification for divorce.

To have a want or preference is an expression of yourself; it is an expression of what you believe is important for you to live well, to have a good life. As such, it's important that your wants and preferences be acknowledged. At the same time, they are not demands that must be catered to, pronto. Wants or preferences are things that you value but are willing to negotiate about, in good faith, with your spouse. From my perspective, my wants (and associated preferences) are the best expression of who I am so long as they are vetted—i.e., carefully and critically examined on a regular basis. My wants stem from my values, my desire to flourish, my gender, and my experiences in life.

Differences between the sexes—to the degree that we know what these are—may be important in determining individual wants of husbands and wives. As wants and preferences, they can be negotiated, avoiding the risk of having gender differences create the opportunity for an unequal relationship by privileging male over female need, or vice versa.

TAKING COLLABORATION SERIOUSLY

———

Before delving into a full account of how to organize your marriage around negotiating your wishes and wants in your marriage, taking a moment to think about what collaboration means and doesn't mean is helpful. To negotiate effectively requires great attention to maintaining a collaborative attitude. Here are some thoughts about what collaboration means:[2]

Collaborators are equal.

True collaborators are always equals. Each partner must accept full responsibility for his/her part in the process of negotiation. Collaboration requires the sharing of authority, accepting personal responsibility, and negotiating in good faith.

Collaboration is not capitulation.

Collaboration protects individual autonomy. Most of us have a (possibly subconscious) fear of being overwhelmed by someone and are reluctant to surrender any part of our autonomy in a relationship. True collaboration does not require this type of surrender.

Collaboration is not cooperation.

Collaboration is about the *process* of working together, while cooperation is about the *result* of working together. For example, I can cooperate with you by stepping aside while you do what you want to do.

A committed marriage is a lifelong partnership that links two people around their most fundamental wishes and wants. An equitable marriage allows the two people involved to flourish as individuals and as a couple. This requires great attention to the maintenance of a collaborative environment of negotiation.

WHEN NEGOTIATION IS NOT COLLABORATIVE

Not all forms of negotiation are collaborative. Such non-collaborative forms of negotiation include:

Compromising.

This may look like collaboration but is more frequently capitulation, building problems for the future.

Competing.

This occurs when both of you are fighting to get your own way using whatever strategy suits you.

Accommodating.

This is a distancing form of compromise. You are basically saying, "I think I can live with that," but you are really separating yourself from the process and your partner.

Avoiding.

This is a common way of not dealing with the process or each other. If you're avoiding, you might say, for example, "I'd rather not talk about this now."

Consent.

This is not negotiation because a great deal of consent may come from hidden coercion in the form of some imbalance in the relationship (e.g., a financial or psychological imbalance).

Collaboration derives from the unique qualities and contribution of the collaborators. If either of you does not participate as a fully engaged and equal partner, it might as well be one person making the decisions.

NEGOTIATING COLLABORATIVELY IS ABOUT COMMITMENT

———

Most people think the idea of commitment between husband and wife is about staying together through thick and thin. This is what is called an aspirational statement—what you believe should and hope will occur in your marriage. This book is about the hard work needed to make this aspiration a reality. The willingness to negotiate issues in good faith with your spouse is so important that I believe it rises to the level of a vow you will be willing to make upon finishing this book.

CHAPTER 1 —————————

TAKEAWAYS

A new, revolutionary approach must be adopted if couples today are to achieve an equitable, sustainable marriage.

Marriage should be organized around negotiating wishes and wants collaboratively.

Marriage can no longer be organized around traditional gender roles.

It is vital to differentiate between the demand quality of needs versus the negotiation quality of wants.

Collaboration between equal partners is neither capitulation nor cooperation.

An equal partnership does not have a managing partner.

Negotiating collaboratively with your spouse is about commitment to the marriage.

2

The Negotiation Process

As I said in Chapter 1, negotiation in marriage is not like negotiating in business, where each party seeks to maximize his/her own gains. Nor is the negotiation process an exchange—a tit-for-tat arrangement. Negotiation in an equitable, committed marriage is a process that begins with sharing with each other the things that are important to you in any given situation—"putting things on the table"—so that you can see if these things are similar or different. If there is a difference or disagreement, negotiation is how you go about resolving the difference or disagreement. Here is a lovely description of the importance of this kind of negotiation process:

> Imagine a family with a free evening and a strong shared wish to spend it together in some form of entertainment. They begin with a number of different proposals, explaining to one another their preferences, the strength of the preferences, the considerations that move them. Each family member learns new things about the character of the various options, and each learns how the others view the possibilities. Nobody wants to do anything that any of the others

regards as too unattractive, and they end up with a plan that reflects their collective wishes. Those collective wishes can't be conceived as the wishes that would emerge from a simple vote in the initial state of mutual ignorance; rather, they are the wishes that would be produced by a more intricate negotiation.[1]

This chapter is about engaging in a negotiation process that promotes this kind of mutual regard and consideration between a husband and wife.

DISAGREEMENTS VS. CONFLICTS

As a psychologist who has worked with couples for many years, I remain adamant about distinguishing between couples having a **disagreement** and couples actually being in **conflict** with one another. Lots of couples, and the people who advise them, use the words disagreement and conflict interchangeably; I, however, believe that doing so ignores important differences between these two types of interactions.

Differences and **disagreements** about what you and your partner want in your relationship will happen. You can disagree about when to go to the movies. You can differ over how to discipline your children. You can differ on when to have sexual relations. You can disagree on where to get the car serviced.

When you disagree with your spouse, it is about *something*.

It's about whether or not you will go to the *movie*; it's about how to *discipline a child*; it's about whether or not you will have *sex tonight*; and it's about where to get the *car serviced*.

The defining thing about a disagreement is that you and your partner are talking to each other. And because you are talking to each other, you can negotiate a resolution of the disagreement. You can look for a win-win outcome; one of you can make an accommodation to the other; or you can agree to disagree with each other and move on. Most important, after the disagreement, you are both still talking to each other.

This is not the case when there is a conflict between you and your spouse. When you are in conflict with one another, you are making assumptions about each other that are hidden, and the feelings you have toward each other are negative and strong. In a conflict, you are not talking; rather, you are yelling, avoiding, talking over each other, etc. In a conflict, the issue will not be resolved because you cannot negotiate. Misunderstandings arise based on the hidden assumptions you are making about each other. There is no benefit to the relationship because there is no resolution of the situation.

In this chapter, I will talk about how to identify when you are in conflict with your partner and how you can go about stopping that conflict. I also want to take you through the process of **self-reflection** about your part in the conflict at hand and how you take personal responsibility for your part —how you can be **personally accountable.** Then I will take you through the negotiation process using a difference that one couple, Sara and Lucas, had about where to park their car.

First, though, let's deal with conflict.

IDENTIFYING WHEN A CONFLICT IS OCCURRING

———

The first clue that you are setting yourself up for conflict with your spouse is how you are feeling. If you feel angry in an interaction with your spouse, you are set to blame him/her —e.g., "I'm **angry** because you are not doing your fair share of the housework." In this situation, something your spouse has done (or failed to do) has "caused" you to feel angry at him/her. You think it is **normal** for you to feel angry at her/him because he/she did not do his/her fair share.

This scenario of thinking your spouse caused you to be angry (or hurt, or fearful, etc.) and then describing this as normal is truly the basis for having a conflict. It is more accurate to describe this type of reaction as "automatic" (reflexive) rather than "normal." Calling such emotional reactions normal is typically used to justify acting on that emotion rather than reflecting on the situation.

Viewing the emotions we have in interpersonal interactions as a physiological reaction caused by something the other person did is the common sense theory of emotion. This is what we are assuming when we think/say, "You made me so angry when you didn't call me." What we are assuming is that emotions are distinct states that have associated distinct brain states—e.g., there is a set of "anger neurons" that are triggered when your spouse does something you don't like.

New research by Lisa Feldman Barrett and her colleagues at the Interdisciplinary Affective Science laboratory at Northeastern University challenges the idea that our emotions are "things" in our brain.[2] They reject the idea that each psychologically identifiable emotion (e.g., anger, fear, hurt) can be identified from your brain's electrical signals, your facial muscle movements, and your bodily changes, such as increased heart rate and sweating. Instead, Feldman Barrett's work indicates that emotions like anger, fear, and happiness are associated with a variety of body and brain states that are dependent upon the context in which they occur and our own personal histories. When you are angry with your spouse, for example, sometimes your heart rate will increase, other times it will decrease, and still other times it will stay the same. You might scowl as you plot your revenge, or you might smile.

If you act when you are feeling angry, hurt, or fearful, you are going to behave badly. What usually happens is you yell, shut down, criticize, or engage in other negative behaviors, which increases the likelihood that your spouse will feel angry, hurt, fearful, etc., in return. **Now you two have a conflict.** Whatever the issue, the conflict is now about how you both are feeling toward each other and the negative assumptions you are making about each other. The issue now is that he is a shirker and she is off on one of her emotional binges. This is now a conflict about who is right, who has injured the other, who is the worse spouse.

HOW TO BE SELF-REFLECTIVE AND PERSONALLY ACCOUNTABLE

The way to resolve conflict is for each person to be **self-re-flective** and **personally accountable** for their part in the breakdown of the interaction at hand.

Being self-reflective, however, is hard work. A recent article in the *Harvard Business Review* eloquently described what being self-reflective is about:

> At its simplest, reflection is about careful thought. But the kind of reflection that is really valuable . . . is more nuanced than that. The most useful reflection involves the conscious consideration and analysis of beliefs and actions for the purpose of learning. Reflection gives the brain an opportunity to pause amidst the chaos, untangle and sort through observations and experiences, consider multiple possible interpretations, and create meaning. This meaning becomes learning, which can then inform future mindsets and actions.[3]

The idea that self-reflection requires conscious consideration is a core task you have in your interactions with your spouse. Here are the steps you can take to allow you to consciously consider your actions.

Being Mad at Your Spouse . . .

. . . is not evidence that he/she has done something wrong. Being angry, afraid, and/or hurt tells you that you're taking something personally. What this means is that your emotional reactions are not giving you a true, unbiased picture of what is happening outside your mind and body. This undermines the idea that when you are angry, afraid, and/or hurt it means your spouse has done something wrong. Maybe he or she has, but you can't tell this from your emotional reaction. This also means that when your spouse is angry at you, it does not necessarily mean you have done something wrong.

This idea is compelling to the spouse on the receiving end of an emotional reaction. I worked with one man who was not assertive in his relationship with his wife. He found this information remarkably helpful . . . the idea that he did not have to be intimidated when his wife was angry at him.

Enhance Your Emotional Intelligence.

Remember that emotions such as anger and fear, along with the catchall emotion of hurt, tell you that you are reacting personally to the situation. Such emotions are associated with the release of the corticotropin-releasing hormone (CHR), along with hormones and neurotransmitters, including epinephrine (adrenaline), norepinephrine, and dopamine, all of which ready you for a fight-or-flight response. Daniel Goleman, who developed the idea of emotional intelligence, views such emotions as a "quick response system" that pushes you to react to a person or situation without appropriate reflection on what is occurring.[4] If you act on these emotions in your marriage, you will not behave well toward your spouse.

Psychiatrist David Viscott describes nicely all the ways we talk about being angry and fearful.[5] Anger can be expressed as being irritated, miffed, teed off, irked, annoyed, furious, enraged, and burned. Fear can be expressed as being scared, edgy, jittery, concerned, worried, helpless, insecure, uptight, nervous, having cold feet, and getting the shakes. Viscott says that being "hurt" is a catchall term that people use to describe all sorts of feeling without admitting to much. What Viscott means is that "feeling hurt" is a vague term that allows us to avoid taking full responsibility for what we are saying. It also tends to implicate someone for causing the hurt. I can feel angry without it necessarily being at someone; same with fear. Not so with hurt. When I am hurt, it is because someone caused it.

Recognize Your Personal Take on the Situation.

Because of the "quick response system" described by Daniel Goleman, you will make a quick interpretation of what is happening between you and your spouse that will be based more on your own history than on the current situation. All of us bring our personal histories (painful and joyful) with us into our marriage. When you react based on your personal history, you're characterizing your spouse's action in terms of what it means to you personally. For example, you come home from work to find that your spouse has not gone grocery shopping on the way home as he/she had agreed to do. Your quick response system goes into action, and you say, "I am so angry that you are not doing your fair share of the work."

Notice that this is a characterization of your spouse's action—or rather, his/her lack of action—as unfair. This is your experience of the situation. Your spouse also has a view of the undone task. Your spouse will rarely, if ever, experience his/her action in the same way that you characterize it. The sense of unfairness in the example is your personal experience of the situation.

Characterizing an action is not the same thing as **describing** it. Here is a schematic showing what is happening to you when you are taking something personally, using the example of your spouse not going to the grocery as planned.

Characterization of Spouse

Triggering Event	⟶	Alarm Reaction	⟶	Characterization of Spouse
Did Not Go to Store	⟶	Angry	⟶	Not Doing "Fair Share"

Remember, this kind of reaction to your spouse is always a comment about the relationship, what is happening between the two of you. It is **never** about the event—e.g., them not going to the store.

LEARN TO DESCRIBE, NOT CHARACTERIZE

Recognize that feeling angry, irritated, peeved, hurt, or annoyed at your spouse indicates that you are reacting automatically. Your first response is to characterize him/her as having some negative trait that caused her/him to act badly (they're selfish, lazy, bossy, messy, thin-skinned, ignores you, etc.). This is not a description of what happened.

Here are a few examples of the difference between **describing** what happens and **characterizing** what happens:

WHAT SPOUSE DID	HOW YOU CHARACTERIZED IT
He/she did not attend to me in the way I wanted	He/she **ignored** me
She/he spent money on things that she/he wanted	She/he is **selfish**
He/she checked his/her phone when we were talking	He/she is so **self-centered**
She/he wants to have sex more often than I do	She/he is a **sex-addict**
He/she did not consider my opinion	He/she treats me like a **second class-citizen**

Once you identify the problem, you can describe it to your spouse, leading the way to a negotiation of a possible disagreement about what happened.

THE NEGOTIATION PROCESS: AN EXAMPLE

Lucas and Sara had a disagreement about where Sara should park when she drove the car to the mall. Lucas did not want Sara to park in the parking garage, which was her preference.

Here are the steps in the negotiation about where Sara will park when she goes to the mall.[6]

First Step: Approaching Your Partner

When you have something on your mind, give your partner a heads-up about what you want to talk about. It is important to give him/her time to think about his/her own thoughts about the issue. Set a time when it is convenient for you both to talk. (In my family, we ask for a consultation about a given issue, concern, want, preference, etc.)

Second Step: Expressing What You Want

This is a disagreement about different **preferences** (wants or desires) that Lucas and Sara have about something that Sara is doing. When you have different preferences about how things should be done, the focus of your conversation should be to discover the concerns and interests each person has around the specific issue. In an open discussion about an issue:

- ✦ Each of you wants to be able to express your perspective on how you see things.
- ✦ Each of you should be able to explain why what you prefer to do is important to you.
- ✦ Each of you should give the other person the opportunity to express his/her preference, without interruption.
- ✦ Watch for hidden personal agendas you may have. If you are feeling anxious or angry, talk about it.

Through open discussion of their concerns around this issue, Sara and Lucas found that they both had good reasons for taking the positions they did. He was concerned about the car getting scratched or dented by other car doors, resulting in repair costs, because the parking spaces in the garage were so narrow. What concerned Sara was finding a convenient parking spot when she was running errands and getting to important engagements, like doctors' appointments, on time.

Third Step: Recognizing That Every Concern of Yours Is a Concern of Mine

Through this discussion, Sara and Lucas demonstrated that "every concern of yours is a concern of mine" (rather than just defending their own position as the right, smart, logical, sensible position). That is, they listened to each other and honored what the other thought was important. Being able to be clear about your specific concerns in each situation and being able to clearly state this concern is important to finding workable solutions to the issue or disagreement.

Final Step: Making a Win-Win Action Plan

The best outcome of this kind of discussion is a win-win action plan that is responsive to the stated concerns. Here is the win-win solution Lucas and Sara achieved: Lucas will drive Sara into town when he is working from home. When she drives herself, she will park on the upper levels of the garage, where there are fewer cars, and take care to park in the middle of the space to decrease the risk of dents from other car doors.

IF IT BECOMES A CONFLICT

———

Sometimes, during your attempt to negotiate an issue, you will find yourself getting annoyed, irritated, etc., or you may find yourself tuning out. Recognize that when this happens to you or your spouse, the two of you are at risk of moving into conflict with each other. If this happens, stop your discussion. Each of you can take the time to assess your own personal reaction to the situation and recoup your serenity; then you can set a time to begin the negotiation process again.

In Appendix B, you will find a list of important issues that you will face in your marriage—issues around which you will want to negotiate. The issues highlighted are goals, lifestyle, finances, children, health/wellness, and sexuality. Included are questions to open discussion for negotiating collaboratively about these areas in your marriage.

THE IMPACT OF NEGOTIATING ON THE QUALITY OF YOUR RELATIONSHIP

———

You may think that negotiating everything is too much to ask of any couple. This reluctance stems in part because we usually think about negotiation as it relates to legal or business interactions. But I am not promoting a transactional relationship, i.e., a relationship in which both partners do things for each other with the expectation of reciprocation. I am promoting a marriage in which both partners are concerned with each other's well-being as well as their own—an interactional marriage.

When collaborative negotiation is written out in this way, in such great detail, it may seem overly formal to you. And when you first begin to incorporate this approach, it may be awkward for you. Over time, that will change. The process will become more familiar, more comfortable, and you will reap the benefits this kind of interaction yields to your relationship.

While the process of negotiation is always intentional, in the sense that you must remain committed to the process, it will be less formal around many of the day-to-day interactions you have. In due time, it will become almost automatic. At the same time, more formal collaborative negotiation is always there if a disagreement or conflict arises, and for the major decisions you face in your marriage.

The benefits of collaborative negotiation within a partnership are:

Gaining Respect for One Another

My husband and I intentionally interact with one another using the process of collaborative negotiation. We have found it indispensable in establishing the kind of marriage I am describing in this book. What we have also found is that engaging in this process over time and many, many events, we have come to gain great respect for each other over and above the love we share. This is one of those unintended consequences of doing the hard work of negotiating collaboratively. I think this respect comes from each of us not only being willing to listen attentively to each other's positions about all aspects of our lives but also actively seeking out such thoughts and feelings. Explaining our preferences to each other, how strong such preferences are, and why a particular preference is important to each of us encourages a deeper understanding of and respect for each other.

Building Trust in Each Other

Another extremely important unintended consequence of having collaborative negotiation as the bedrock of your marriage is that it builds a new kind of trust between the two of you. Most people think of trust as a character trait of the individual. I take a different position. I believe trust is a process that occurs in three stages: trust in one's self, trust in the process of collaborative negotiation, and trust in your partner.

- *Trust in Yourself.* Trust in yourself comes from the self-reflective journey I will ask you to take in Chapters 3 and 4. Becoming increasingly self-aware of your own issues and insecurities, and learning to manage them, brings about this trust in yourself. That is, you learn you can get through uncomfortable, hard, unpleasant events that can happen in life. And you do this with someone you love and who is there to help you.

- *Trust in the Negotiation Process.* As you organize your relationship around negotiating collaboratively, you learn you can rely on this process to be heard, to be understood, to be valued, and to solve life's difficulties—and you can see that your spouse is also invested in this process.

✦ *Trust in Your Partner.* By learning to trust yourself and trust the negotiation process as the way to interact with your partner, over time you will increasingly view your partner as a trustworthy person (in the common-sense view of trust). This idea of trust is something you can cultivate with your partner. You do not need to rely on the idea that you must pick a partner who already has some desirable trait. The two of you build trust together. Respect and trust for one another is achieved through the hard work of negotiating collaboratively with one another over the course of your marriage.

CHAPTER 2 ———————————

TAKEAWAYS

The process of collaboratively negotiating issues and disagreements is what enhances your marital relationships and secures its sustainability.

Disagreements are not conflicts. Disagreements can be negotiated. Conflicts require self-reflection and personal accountability.

There are steps you can take to become more self-aware and personally accountable.

You can negotiate win-win solutions to differences if you are not in conflict.

You and your partner's respect for and trust of one another will be enhanced through collaborative negotiation.

PART II

———

THE PERSONAL
REVOLUTION

3

————

Taking Care of Your
Personal Issues

Self-reflection is the conscious consideration and analysis of your actions for the purpose of increasing your ability to negotiate collaboratively with your spouse. As I noted earlier, self-reflection is the opportunity you take in your everyday life to pause and sort through your experiences in your marriage in order to be a more effective spouse.

This chapter looks at what taking things personally means in a marriage. Taking something personally is how we commonly describe a reflexive reaction that is driven by the need to protect our own ego. This is a natural response—but when you are protecting yourself psychologically, you do not have empathy and concern for your spouse that you need to have in order to interact with them kindly, thoughtfully, considerately, and effectively. And this sets up a situation in which conflict between the two of you becomes likely.

In Chapter 2, I used the example of your spouse having failed to go the grocery store on the way home after saying they would go as an example of a situation that can trigger a personal, reflexive reaction. Be aware that any situation can be a trigger for a personal reaction at one time or another, and that's because your reaction comes more from your personal history than from the current situation. This chapter is about how to consciously consider and analyze what is happening to you when you are taking things personally.

TAKING THINGS PERSONALLY

———

Let's start with a few everyday interactions between a husband and wife that are excellent examples of one or both taking something personally:

- ✦ "How can you ignore me like that? I work so hard at being nice to you." . . . "I don't know what you're talking about."
- ✦ "I can't believe you're checking the sports scores when we wanted to spend time together watching TV!" . . . "It will only take a second; don't get so upset over such a little thing."
- ✦ "My opinion doesn't count, I feel like a second-class citizen in this relationship." . . . "Oh, here we go again, I can't do anything right."
- ✦ "You spend so much money on things that are not important; you're so selfish." . . . "I work hard, and it is my money."
- ✦ "You never want to have sex." . . . "You just want it all the time, you're a sex addict."

Interactions like these always involve one or both partners taking things personally. In the above brief scenarios, one or both of you are feeling angry, hurt, frustrated, upset, anxious, etc., and are accusing, blaming, yelling, criticizing, calling the other names, etc. Most marriage counselors know that people cannot negotiate a win-win solution to a problem in this state. Typically, they will tell you to step back and cool off. But simply cooling off is not good enough. During that break, you also need to consciously consider what is happening to you psychologically when this kind of interaction happens so that you can feel better, learn to defuse such defensive reactions, and begin to problem solve.

Let's examine the first scenario described above. Lucas, the husband, probably did not listen attentively to something Sara (his wife) was saying. She characterizes his action as ignoring her, and follows up with a self-serving statement about her own niceness. This, of course, is intended to bolster the way she experiences Lucas's action; after all, she is accusing him of not being nice to her.

While she doesn't say it directly here, Sara is likely feeling angry and/or hurt. Feeling ignored is a **Sara-issue** because she is feeling personally discounted.

As we discussed in Chapter 2, Sara is characterizing Lucas's action, not describing it. A description of Lucas's action would be something like, "Lucas, I'm not sure you are listening to what I am saying," or, "Lucas, I want to have some time together. I am not sure that is what you want." This approach identifies a relationship issue: *how* Lucas is interacting with Sara. It is not about Sara feeling discounted.

While Lucas did not respond to Sara in a way that is important to her (listening to her when she wanted him to do so or spending time with her), her characterization of his action as ignoring her is personal. Lucas, meanwhile, was not deliberately trying to ignore Sara and is likely caught off guard by the accusation, so he dismisses what she is saying ("I don't know what you're talking about"), either in self-defense or for self-protection (now it is also a **Lucas-issue**). Thus, Sara's concern does not get addressed because both parties are now defending their positions. Whatever the issue started as, it is now about how Lucas and Sara are feeling toward each other, the negative assumptions they are making about each other, and the negative things they may be saying to each other. Now it is about the relationship, not the issue. Now Sara and Lucas have a **conflict**, not a problem—which means they can't discuss and resolve things through negotiation.

Taking something personally happens when you portray your partner's action *only* in terms of how you experience it. How you experience your spouse's action, while important to you, is not the only way to describe the action.

Psychologists describe what is happening to you when you are taking something personally as you feeling **threatened.** People often refer to this kind of feeling as **being insecure.** It feels like your pride, self-esteem, sense of security, or sense of personal worth is being challenged. Saying you're feeling insecure may be an ill-defined description of not being good enough in some way—not important enough, not smart enough, not respected enough, not good-looking enough, not sexy enough, what have you.

What is most important for you to understand and accept in this kind of situation is that it is **your interpretation of your spouse's action** (inaction), not the actual problem, that causes your feeling of threat or insecurity. His/her action, while a problem for you, is not the threat.

In Appendix C, you will find a "Taking Things Personally

Worksheet" that you can use to better understand your own insecurities. I use the example of Sara feeling ignored by Lucas as the example of how to use this worksheet. Sara starts out entering how she experienced the event with Lucas— what she felt and what she did (she **got angry** when she experienced what Lucas did as **ignoring** her, followed by yelling that he was **being inconsiderate** of her). The next part of filling out the worksheet is to reflect on **describing** (not her automatic reaction) what Lucas did. In this case, he **did not pay attention to Sara in the way she wanted him to.** What Sara can learn from this part of the task is that describing the facts of an event is significantly, importantly different from describing the way she experienced it.

The next step, which is a big one, in completing this worksheet is to reflect upon how feeling ignored is a personal threat to Sara. Also in Appendix C, I provide a strategy called "The Downward Arrow" that Sara can use to help her understand the personal threat she experienced when Lucas did not attend to her in the way she wanted him to.[1]

Using this worksheet regularly will help you deal with your insecurities in your marriage, which can profoundly enhance your ability to be an effective partner.

WHAT WE CAN LEARN FROM RATS ABOUT FEELING THREATENED

Rats are one of the animals psychologists use to test one theory of how learning occurs. A major finding of this approach to how we learn things is what is called "escape and avoidance learning." **Escape** conditioning refers to the situation in which a rat learns to "escape" a noxious stimulus, i.e., a rat learns to jump off an electrified platform into water when a shock is turned on. This is the "get me out of here" or "shut this thing off" response.

The rat can learn quickly that it can **avoid** being shocked if it jumps off the electrified platform before the shock is turned on, when it gets a cue that the shock is coming. Avoidance behaviors are incredibly persistent; they continue to happen long after there is no longer anything to avoid. The rat will jump off the platform at the sound of the cue long after the shock generator is turned off, even if the experimenter never turns it on again. What keeps the avoidance behavior going is the **relief** the rat experiences as it jumps off the platform.

We humans demonstrate a similar escape-avoidance kind of learning in the face of a noxious (highly unpleasant) situation. Our human noxious stimulus is feeling threatened in an interpersonal situation. Feeling threatened, usually signaled by feeling angry, irritated, miffed, hurt, anxious, and/or fearful, is the dreaded sense of being exposed as inadequate in some way.

Sara being triggered by Lucas not responding to her in the way she wanted is analogous to the **noxious stimulus**. Sara felt threatened, and her automatic reaction was to accuse Lucas of ignoring her. Holding Lucas responsible for her experience, expecting him to change—i.e., getting rid of the noxious stimulus—was Sara's way of escaping. In situations in which you find yourself feeling threatened, you can learn to recognize your escape responses. You will either do something to "shut this thing off" (blame your spouse for what is happening) or to "get me out of here" (shut down verbally or leave the room).

Like the rats in those experiments, we develop strategies designed to **avoid noxious situations** with our partners that feel threatening to us. These strategies are typically identified as defenses—and it's no wonder we develop such self-protective strategies; we do not want to continually have to escape experiences that cause us to feel insecure or inadequate, and to behave so badly toward our spouses.

Early on in life, we develop **subconscious patterns** that we use to avoid threatening feelings of not being good enough in some way. The early forms of these defenses morph into adult self-protective strategies. These well-entrenched strategies become the way we try to manage situations to avoid a sense of threat or feeling of insecurity.

I prefer the term "self-protective strategies" to "defenses" because most people associate that word with the common Freudian (Anna, not Sigmund) defenses of denial, repression, regression, projection, intellectualization, rationalization, and sublimation. These defenses are used to protect our self from our self (our ego from our id). The strategies I am identifying here, in contrast, are the ones we use to protect our self from **perceived** attack, criticism, rejection, etc. from our spouse.

Here are a few examples of self-protective strategies and how we rationalize them:

SELF-PROTECTIVE STRATEGIES

STRATEGY	INTERPERSONAL GOAL	RATIONALE
CONTROL	I direct, manage, determine what my spouse does in order not to feel vulnerable.	I assume authority because of some attribute (e.g., being male/female) or status (breadwinner/homemaker)
INGRATIATION	I seek to anticipate and adjust to my spouse's perceived wants by not stating my own wants in order not to feel like a burden.	I am a nice and caring person.
PERFECTIONISM	I try to avoid error in order not to be corrected or criticized.	Doing things "correctly," "logically," "the right way."
WITHDRAWAL	I avoid discussing or negotiating issues so I don't have to change, or get run over.	I am just a quiet person; I don't want to argue.
CRITICISM	I take a judgmental approach toward my spouse to feel capable, in control.	I am just being factual.
BEING OVER-RESPONSIBLE	I assume responsibility for my spouse's feelings and actions so I don't feel guilty.	I just want you to have the things you want.
BEING COMPLIANT	I give in to perceived demands to avoid feeling like a burden or avoid criticism.	I am being nice, helpful, accommodating.
DRIVENESS	I focus on my success to the detriment of my marriage, my spouse, and myself to feel important, valued.	I am just doing my job.

HOW ESCAPE AND AVOIDANCE TACTICS PLAY OUT IN YOUR RELATIONSHIP

As I described earlier in this chapter, Sara accused Lucas of ignoring her when he did not respond to her in the way she wanted. Lucas responded in a dismissive way, saying that he did not know what she was talking about. This pattern of interaction can occur over and over in a marriage without either partner ever identifying the problems they're trying to address because they end up in conflict, and conflict is not resolvable. It's impossible to find a solution with your partner when neither one of you is dealing with the issue (not being attended to in a way you like, checking sports scores when having time together, partner not listening, determining how money is spent, solving differences in interest in sex, etc.). You both are dealing with your personalized reactions to each other and trying to escape feeling badly by blaming the other. Marital conflict is the result of trying to escape, rather than dealing with, perceived threatening situations and obnoxious actions.

Your self-protective strategies detract from your ability to engage effectively with your spouse. Trying to manage your own sense of insecurity by directing, maneuvering, or changing your spouse is neither psychologically healthy nor effective. When you are in a self-protective mode, you do not have the capacity to engage in a positive interaction; you do not want to negotiate. The problem is, we do not typically acknowledge our self-protective strategies. Rather, we rationalize them as legitimate interpersonal actions.

MANAGING ESCAPE AND AVOIDANCE STRATEGIES

———

Personal insecurities that elicit escape tactics are not set in stone. Don't waste your time trying to overcome or get rid of them. What you can do, however, is manage and modify your personal insecurities—through some effort on your part. Here are some suggestions for how to do this:

Regularly Take a Personal Inventory.

Using the "Taking Things Personally Worksheet" in Appendix C, keep a journal of the kinds of insecurities that tend to show up in your inventories. They will emerge under the inventory heading of "What is the threat to me?" As you begin to recognize such themes of insecurity occurring when you are interacting with your spouse, try to stop the automatic escape action. Take a time-out when you recognize that you are reacting rather than interacting so that you can remind yourself of your own worth. Once you reestablish your own worth, you can address the issue or problem you are concerned about, e.g., Sara being concerned about how interested Lucas is in her.

Identify Where the Insecurities Come From.

Ask yourself, "How old is this particular feeling of not being ___ enough?" (Smart enough, responsible enough, lovable enough, valuable enough, important enough, sexy enough, etc.) You'll find you can trace many such feelings back to some childhood experience(s). What is your picture of your-self at this earlier age? What were the circumstances when you felt this early threat? What were you feeling in that situ-ation: afraid, angry, hurt, or scared? Can you remember or figure out how you interpreted the disturbing situation that you are examining? Did you feel not good enough? Not smart enough? Like you weren't fitting in? Were you being a burden? Were you powerless? Weren't acceptable? (More about this in Chapter 4!)

Honor and Embrace Your Insecurities.

Remember, we all suffer from such feelings of inadequacy. This is not a sign of some psychological malady or impair-ment. I have used the concept of the inner child to address individual insecurities with clients. I don't use this concept as some form of semi-independent mental agent like the ego, however. Instead, I use this notion informally, treating it as a metaphor for the remnants of early experience. This is a way of talking about emotion-driven residuals of early experience that can be triggered in the current moment.

I suggest we recognize and honor such remnants; they represent an aspect of our lived experience. We cannot and should not want to be rid of these experiences; we cannot cure ourselves of them. Instead, we must honor and manage them. Here is one person's compassionate self-talk to manage such remnants:

I see you, insecurity, and I acknowledge you're there. I
let myself feel the sting of you instead of avoiding the
feeling altogether, no matter how bad it feels, because

*feeling you allows me to have peace with you. It means
I'm human. It means I'm alive. It means I can empathize
with those around me. And most of all, it means that if
I have the ability to feel so negatively about myself, I
most definitely have the ability to feel so positively
about myself.*[2]

Recognize Your Self-Protective Strategies.

Of course, the first step in managing your self-protective
strategies is to recognize what they are. You have developed
these strategies to help you avoid feelings of insecurity, but
they are ineffective and unhealthy long-term approaches to
your issues. Look at the **Rationale** column of the list of self-
protective strategies I shared earlier in this chapter. This column describes the way you think about yourself, e.g., "I am a
quiet person" or "I am a nice person." You are likely to think
that the rationalization you are using for a particular strategy
or strategies are due to your temperament or personality.
Temperament and personality are seen as a basic, inherent
part of people, so we don't think of trying to change them.
Perhaps these traits—being quiet or being nice—truly are
characteristic of you. Even so, you should not use them as a
way of trying to maneuver or manage your spouse.

Self-Reflection Is the Key.

Become more willing to be self-reflective by both recognizing when you are taking things personally and recognizing
the patterns of self-protection that you use to avoid feeling
insecure and/or inadequate. The payoffs—to you personally
and to your relationship—will be dramatic. When you first

make the attempt to be more self-reflective, it will seem awkward and you will feel quite self-absorbed. Over time, however, you will learn new approaches to communicating interpersonally with your spouse, and as those become more second nature, your old patterns will require less attention.

Seek Out Talking Therapy.

Get assistance from a nonjudgmental person or professional to help you understand, embrace, and manage your feelings of insecurity. Remember, when you are reacting personally to current situations, the current situation is likely triggering a young (I don't like calling the reaction "childish"; that's too critical sounding for me) feeling that deserves examination.

CHAPTER 3 ————————

T
A
K
E
A
W

A
Y
S

Self-reflection is basic to recognizing when you are taking things personally.

When you take things personally (when you escape or avoid a perceived threat), you will characterize your spouse rather than describe what is happening.

Your spouse may agree with your description of the situation, but he/she is unlikely to agree with how you are characterizing her/him.

Self-protective strategies are not personally healthy and do not promote the well-being of the relationship.

Be willing to do the work to recognize and manage your insecurities (i.e., the things that will be psychological threats to you).

Be willing to identify and own up to the self-protective strategies you use with your spouse.

We all suffer from such feelings; this is not a sign of some psychological malady or impairment.

4

Where Do Insecurities Come From?

Feeling threatened is about having some vague sense of inadequacy or fear of a perceived flaw being exposed. It is this—the dreaded sense of exposure of perceived flaws—that is the very essence of feeing threatened, in fact.

There is ample evidence that childhood experiences are recorded in some form in our memory, and those memories can be evoked in our adult interactions. Such experiences are frequently evoked in our adult intimate relationships because we expect extra consideration from our spouse. Married couples are vulnerable to experiencing a dreaded feeling of not being good enough, important enough, recognized enough, valued enough, or worthy. These feelings come from our own sense of vulnerability or insecurity, and we all suffer from them at one time or another. It is a consequence of the cognitive and emotional limitations of childhood.

Let's use "feeling ignored" as an example of how we can be affected by earlier childhood experience. To understand the experience of being ignored, we must think about a child's experience of **not being paid attention to in a way he/she wants.**

Let's imagine a child in the following situation with his dad.[1] One Sunday the child's dad is enjoying reading the newspaper, preoccupied with what he wants to do. His son approaches and interrupts him, asking him to play a game with him; he wants some attention. The dad is preoccupied and responds to the boy in a sharp tone, "Can't you see I'm busy? Don't bother me."

This is not abuse, this is not awful; it's an adult being interested in something he wants to do and prioritizing his wants over his son's. Perhaps he's usually attentive, but in this moment he needs some alone time.

Children experience events such as this one entirely differently from how adults experience them. Children are utterly dependent, both physically and emotionally, on their parents for the fulfillment of their needs and wants. Children cannot be objective about themselves; they're not self-aware enough to know that they are okay even if they are in trouble or aren't getting what they need or want. They cannot evaluate how they are doing in the world separately from how they think others see them, particularly their parents. **This inability to think objectively about oneself is a characteristic of childhood cognition.** Children's reliance on others is their natural dependency on adults, particularly parents.

The boy in this example experiences his father's lack of acknowledgment of his wish as a rejection; he thinks his father is saying that something is wrong with him. Otherwise, he reasons, his father would pay attention to him when he asked. It is **as if** the child is saying to himself, "If there weren't something wrong with me or what I want, I would have been attended to." **The child is thinking personally; he**

believes this disappointment must be about him as a person. Of course, his father, like lots of parents, has forgotten how personally children think and, therefore, has failed to realize how his child is experiencing the interaction with him. Over time, with repeated, uncorrected experiences like this, the child can develop a generalized experience of not being good enough—of not being worthy.

By the way, responding appropriately to children does not mean either immediate or even delayed gratification of their request. It does mean openly acknowledging the want and making the child feel that it is important. This acknowledgment of the child's want supports his own feeling of being valued and important, i.e., being "enough" as a human being. To not be attended to, to not have what you want acknowledged, is to be ignored—and to a child, that's personal! In this situation, the father can correct the problem by simply acknowledging his son's wish to have some time with his dad. He can explain his wish to have time to read the newspaper and let his son know he will spend time with him later. He can also apologize for the unkind tone he took toward his child.

HOW CHILDREN MAY EXPERIENCE THEIR PARENTS

———

These kinds of incidences happen to children all the time. As children experience anxiety, fear, and/or anger in such events, their minds and bodies prepare them to protect themselves from the threat of rejection, humiliation, criticism, ridicule, and/or harm. I'm about to share a few examples of how children may experience various kinds of interactions with their parents. These are not what we would label as abusive or severely neglectful situations. Often parents are not wholly aware of the negative impact of their actions or attitudes on their child.

Some examples include:

+ **Critical Parents.** Parents who are overtly evaluative of their children, particularly in a negative manner that undermines their child's sense of competence and their sense of having personal worth. As an adult, this child may well see criticism when it is not intended.

+ **Parent-Child Mismatch.** Parent and child may be temperamentally different. An extroverted parent with an introverted child may result in the child feeling like an "odd duck," as not quite fitting in.

+ **Learning Problems.** Children with learning difficulties, including attention deficit hyperactivity disorder (ADHD), are likely to experience themselves as a burden to their parents. Parents often have a difficult time effectively parenting children with these limitations.

+ **Being Overprotective.** A child with overprotective parents may end up feeling that he isn't able to manage life effectively. He/she may come to rely on others too much for guidance.

+ **Being Part of a Large Family.** Being a child among many children may generate feelings of being a burden and/or not being important. Parents may inadvertently express difficulty about expenses, etc.

+ **Being Put in an Adult Role.** A child who takes on adult responsibility too young is likely to feel simultaneously overly responsible and inadequate to the task at hand as an adult.

+ **Having an Older Sibling Who "Messes Up."** This situation can create internal pressure to be a good boy or girl, creating anxiety whenever the child does not perform or behave well. An example would be having an addicted sibling.

As children, we develop automatic ways of managing these threat-producing situations, which morph into the adult interpersonal strategies described in the previous chapter. The best way to deal with these ineffective strategies is to recognize what they are, when they are likely to emerge, and how to manage them. There is great value in taking a regular personal inventory using the "Taking Things Personally Worksheet" in Appendix C. As we discussed earlier, it's helpful to keep a journal of the kinds of insecurities that tend to show up in your inventories. They will emerge under the inventory heading of "What Is the Threat?" Once you can recognize such themes of insecurity, you will manage them more effectively.

"THEY DID THE BEST THEY COULD."

———

This is the usual reaction of clients I have seen over the years when we've talked about their early difficult childhood experiences. This is the appropriate comment, looking back from the more objective view of the adult. However, what I remind them of is that their experience of these difficult experiences as a child is worth examining. It is the *child's* understanding of and reaction to the difficult events that is important in understanding what is happening when we are taking things personally. You can both be open to looking at the impact of your early experiences on your current interactions with your spouse *and* taking the adult position of an understanding and forgiving, if necessary, attitude toward your parents.

All of us can both identify with and understand the reaction of the father wanting to have time to himself to enjoy the Sunday paper. We can also, with some effort, recall what it was like to be the child when a parent reacted negatively toward us. The goal of looking at the impact of your early experience on your current reactions is to better understand and manage those reactions, not to attack your parents.

CHAPTER 4 ———

T
A
K
E
A
W
A
Y
S

Accountability in your marriage means knowing when you are taking things personally.

Early experiences can intrude upon us in adulthood, often in the form of feeling insecure about something.

Be willing to do the work to recognize your insccurities, which are manageable—if you put forth some effort.

Recognize the self-protective strategies you use with your spouse; doing this enhances your ability to negotiate issues that will continually arise in your marriage.

PART III

THE REVOLUTION
IN THE BEDROOM

5

Enjoying Sex

The challenge you have in the bedroom is to cocreate your own sexual relationship. This is uncharted territory in the twenty-first century. Creating and maintaining an enjoyable sex life in your marriage means understanding what sex means to you personally. To look at sex from this point of view—your individual psychology—is a much-needed alternative to the typical "how-to" manuals that are prevalent today, particularly online. And now that you've worked through Chapters 3 and 4 and begun to address your own personal issues, you're prepared for this approach!

You must be suspicious of being guided by a gendered view of male and female sexual desire when it comes to your interactions with your partner in the bedroom. Free yourself from a too-restrictive view of sex. In the pages to come, I will take on evolutionary psychologists' highly gendered, constraining view of male and female desire to help you do this. I will also raise the issue of the impact of pornography on sex in marriage. You must be thoughtful about if and how this activity plays out in your sexual relationship with your spouse.

CREATING AND MAINTAINING AN EROTIC SEXUAL RELATIONSHIP

—

In Chapter 1, I talked about how a revolutionary marriage is one in which you and your spouse maintain a **simultaneous perspective** of yourselves, both as individuals and as a couple, one in which you preserve the sense of "being in this together" while at the same time having individual life plans.

Esther Perel, a couples' therapist, writes thoughtfully and intelligently about sex in her 2007 book, wonderfully titled *Mating in Captivity*, which is about maintaining a vibrant sexual relationship for the long haul of marriage.[1] Perel talks about having to maintain this simultaneous perspective in order to sustain a lively sex life throughout your marriage. She reminds us that the togetherness or commitment we seek in marriage provides us with a sense of safety and stability in our lives, and notes that we foster this togetherness through various means—creating rituals, habits, and pet names, for example—all of which bring the reassurance that we are loved and valued. Independence and autonomy, on the other hand, is about adventure and excitement. One way we express this adventure and excitement in our marriage is through sex. Thus, we have the tension between autonomy, which thrives on excitement and risk, and commitment, which thrives on the comfort and stability of togetherness.

Taking the simultaneous perspective in your sexual relationship is represented in the image below:

Simultaneous Perspective in Your Erotic Relationship

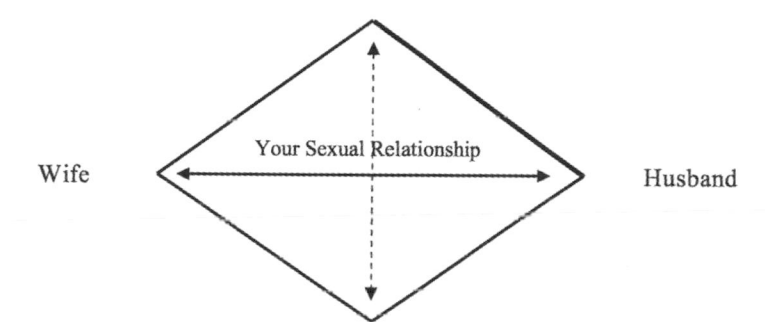

Safety And Security That Comes With Togetherness

Wife — Your Sexual Relationship — Husband

Adventure and Excitement That Comes with
Independence/Autonomy

This schematic depicts the idea that there is a tension or balance that needs to be maintained between togetherness in your marriage, which brings a sense of security and stability to your lives, and maintaining your independence from one another, which allows for excitement and adventure in your lives. The vertical dotted line represents the simultaneous perspective of being together as a couple while also maintaining some independence as individuals. Remember, if one or both of you place too much emphasis on your independence and autonomy, you will be less willing to negotiate the important areas of your life, like your sexual relationship. If you overload on togetherness, in contrast, you can lose the excitement you want in your sexual relationship (i.e., it is likely to become less interesting and less fun).

As Perel says, the need for sexual adventure and excitement is hard to generate with the person you look to for comfort and stability. In fact, generating sexual excitement in marriage can make for a certain amount of insecurity between the two of you. The challenge you have in your marriage is how you manage your conflicting wishes for security/reassurance and the excitement of having a vibrant sexual relationship. Here are several ideas that can help you to find the right balance for you and your spouse:

Dismantle Your Security System.

This is the clever way Perel encourages us to value and respect each other's autonomy.[2] You don't need to cultivate separateness in your early relationship, because at that point you are still quite separate. In the early years of your marriage, eroticism helps you generate closeness; however, in time it is this closeness that you so wanted that can come to inhibit desire. We often seek a peaceful contentment in marriage through the increasing familiarity with each other that comes with time. Our ability to tolerate our separateness, along with the insecurity that it brings, is a precondition for maintaining interest and desire in your relationship. Separateness in marriage is keeping a sense of selfhood. So, instead of putting too much stock in the security and safety of closeness in your marriage, use it to embolden yourself to take the risk to act on your professional ambitions, to confront personal issues, and to take, as Perel suggests, the skydiving course you never dared consider before.

Keep Fresh Eyes.

Keeping fresh eyes is another of Perel's clever ways of telling you that you will enhance eroticism in your marriage by remembering that your spouse is not just a spouse; he/she is also an independent person.[3] One way to do this is to work hard to remember those moments early in your relationship when you were excited by and idealized your new spouse. Our tendency is to think about our spouse in terms of what we want from them, not so much as an independent, autonomous person. In Mating in Captivity, Perel tells the story of a woman who went to a business meeting with her husband and, seeing him acting in this different context, remembered how excited by and admiring of him she was when they first met.

Laura and Mitch

Laura describes Mitch as the classic sex-obsessed man, demanding his rights to sex regardless of how she feels. She complains resentfully that the only time he wants to get close to her is when he wants sex, and he wants it all the time. She values verbal communication as the way to connect. Mitch only knows how to connect through sex, when he feels free and uninhibited. Mitch sees Laura as a sexually inhibited woman who repeatedly rejects his advances with feelings of disgust and contempt.

For Laura, sex carries the sum of all the cultural and familial restrictions on women she has absorbed over her lifetime. She grew up believing she could be smart or pretty, but not both. Mitch was a late bloomer, gawky and not particularly athletic. He had two things going for him during adolescence. He was a good dancer and he genuinely liked girls. Mitch's seeking closeness primarily through sex is the residual of his own early experiences.

Laura must battle, like many women, the age-old repressions of female sexuality in which they are trapped in passivity, dependent on men to seduce them. She will want to explore her own capacity for and enjoyment of sex. Mitch must learn to become verbally open about describing what sex means to him to counter how Laura sees him.

Mating in Captivity by Esther Perel (Harper, 2007)

Know Your Own Personal Insecurities.

A major theme of this book is the idea that in order to create and sustain a satisfying and equitable marriage, you must become more self-reflective and less reactive to each other. This is true when it comes to creating and maintaining a vibrant sexual relationship that can last. Sexual difficulties in marriage are often grounded in our own personal issues or insecurities. Since both people have such insecurities, a negative dynamic between spouses often plays out in the couple's sexual relationship. The story of Laura and Mitch (see sidebar) shows how individual insecurities and gender stereotypes can negatively affect a couple's sexual relationship.[4] Here are several ways in which personal issues can get in the way of achieving a satisfactory sex life in the context of a committed marriage:

+ *Sex Is Dirty.*[5] Maria was raised in a family in which sex was never talked about and was considered a sin if you were not married (but you did it anyway). For Maria, it was hard to be open and free about sex and emotionally connected to her spouse.

+ *Anxiety About Commitment.* Women who have not been supported in achieving their own goals may view marriage as having to sacrifice those goals. Men may see marriage as a life sentence of boring sex with one person.

+ *I Won't Be Like My Father.*[6] Steven's father abandoned his mother, who then swore to never let anyone hurt her like that again. Steven found himself passively ducking his wife's sexual advances because of his lack of interest in sex and his unreliable erections. For Steven, emotional safety and security required guarding against his selfish and aggressive inclinations, i.e., guarding against becoming an "asshole" like his father. The closer he got to Rita, the greater the need for caution and the more inhibited he was sexually.

+ *All Feelings Are a Sign of Weakness.*[7] Dylan finds emotional security altogether impossible, with or without sexual excitement. At his mother's funeral when he was twelve, his eyes filled with tears over his great loss. His father said, "I hope you're not going to fall apart on me." Out of fear of rejection by his father, Dylan had to suppress his entire emotional life. For Dylan, all feelings were a sign of weakness in his house. When he starts to have feelings for someone, he feels self-loathing.

Be open to the idea that you may bring fears, unwelcome thoughts, early difficult experiences around sex (including sexual abuse), and/or a distorted view about sex to your relationship. Be willing to talk with your spouse about such events. If you think such experiences are significantly and negatively affecting your ability to cocreate the kind of wonderful, enhancing sexual relationship with your spouse you desire, seek professional help quickly—don't wait!

REMEMBER: IT'S "PREFERENCES," NOT "NEEDS"

Previously I have talked about how prevalent the idea is that in marriage you must fulfill each other's needs. Again, the idea that "needs-that-must-be-fulfilled" is how to organize your marriage promotes a self-centered approach. Of course, we all desire sex, and engaging in sexual activity certainly is fundamental to being human. But how we carry out that sexual desire is through our sexual preferences (what, when, where, how, how frequently). In marriage, we have preferences for the way in which we fulfill our sexual desires—and we must negotiate those preferences.

Couples have relied on the idea that sexual preferences are sexual needs because it allows them to avoid the risk involved in working with their partner to achieve a mutually satisfying sexual relationship. Your wants and preferences must be acknowledged as standing on their own, and being able to negotiate your sexual preferences is important to not just your sexual well-being but your overall well-being. At the same time, **they are not demands that must be catered to.**

THE GENDERED VIEW OF DESIRE

To the evolutionary psychologist, men's sexual inclinations are biologically driven reproductive strategies designed to spread his genes as far as possible. Women, on the other hand, are driven by a biological need to enforce monogamy (via marriage) on men to assure their own and their offspring's chances of survival. These reproductive strategies become the basis for assuming significantly different traits in men and women.

Thank goodness, a growing number of female scientists are venturing into the field of female sexuality, an historically male-dominated field. None of these women scientists are claiming that women's sexual desire, arousal, and orgasm are exactly like men's, of course. Rather, they are arguing that women have a stronger sex drive than was commonly thought in the past. These researchers are challenging modern stereotypes of female sexuality, such as:

+ Women's sex drive is lower than men's.
+ Women are aroused by love, not sex.
+ Women are not naturally sex agents but responders.
+ Women are not as interested in new and different partners as men.

One group of researchers at the University of Michigan, led by Terri Conley, reviewed various theoretical and research approaches to gender differences in sexuality to shed light on the prevalent misconceptions noted above.[8] Here are a selected few of their findings:

Do Women Desire and Have Fewer Sexual Partners Than Men? Bottom Line: No. When women thought that their true sexual history could be revealed by a polygraph (nonfunctional for purposes of the research), differences in numbers of reported sexual partners disappeared.

Do Women Orgasm Less Frequently Than Men? Bottom Line: Yes, But. The orgasm gap (men experience more orgasms than women) diminishes greatly when sex occurs in committed relationships. It may disappear entirely when committed partners "are more generous in providing non-coital sexual attention ('foreplay' or clitoral stimulation)." Woman reach orgasm about 25 percent of the time from intercourse alone.

Do Men Like Casual Sex More Than Do Women? Bottom Line: Yes, But. A greater willingness to engage in casual sex is one of the largest documented sexual gender differences. This discrepancy evaporated when women subjects considered sexual offers from attractive or famous individuals. Women were equally likely as men to accept offers of casual sex from close friends whom they perceived to have high sexual capabilities (thought would provide them with "a positive sexual experience"). Conley concluded from her findings that the only consistently significant predictor that women will accept a proposal of casual sex is the perception that the one who is making the proposal is sexually capable (i.e., will be "good in bed"). Conley also found indirect evidence in her work that women are less interested in casual sex because they perceive greater personal risk than men do in this kind of sexual encounter.

Considering the reviewed research and their own research, Conley and her colleagues suggest that gender differences in sexual behavior—which, though they are the bread and butter of evolutionary psychologists, are *not* biologically rooted in our evolutionary past—stem from much more mundane causes:

- Stigma against women for expressing sexual desires
- Women's socialization to attend to others' needs rather than their own
- A double standard that dictates different sets of appropriate sexual behaviors for men and women

This story of the libidinous male and the sexually indifferent female doesn't make sense anymore . . . it is too rigid and limits the way in which you can coconstruct your own sexual life. You do not have to rely on stereotypical sexual scripts. So don't!

MANGLED SCIENCE ABOUT GENDER AND SEX DIFFERENCES

———

A good example of a popularized, mangled story about sex in marriage that is relevant to our discussion is a *New York Times Magazine* article entitled "Does a More Equal Marriage Mean Less Sex?" that went viral in 2014.[9] This is a catchy title, of course, and the piece got a lot of popular press.

The research upon which this article is based is a research project reported in the 2013 edition of *American Sociological Review*. The researchers reported that for couples in which men did what the researchers defined as "feminine" chores like folding laundry, cooking, or vacuuming, they had sex 1.5 fewer times per month than couples with husbands who completed more "masculine" chores like taking out the garbage or fixing the car. The study also reported that the more traditional the division of labor (the more the husband did masculine as compared to feminine chores), the more sexual satisfaction the wife reported.

Critics of the research point out that the study was based on data collected in 1987 and 1992—more than a generation ago, a time when traditional marriages were the norm. In other words, these findings may support the view that sexual arousal for heterosexual couples of this era was dependent upon traditional gender roles, but much has changed since then, and the data can't necessarily be applied to modern couples.

Using more recent data from a 2006 marital and relationship survey of six hundred married and cohabiting, low-to-moderate income couples with children, Dan Carlson and his colleagues at Georgia State University conducted another study.[10] Their research suggested that the shift toward more egalitarian sharing of housework did not radically undermine sexual intimacy in these couples' relationship. They found that couples with more egalitarian divisions of housework did somewhat better with regard to sexual frequency, satisfaction with sexual frequency, and reports of the quality of their sexual relationships than conventional couples. These egalitarian couples were also substantially happier with the division of labor around the house compared to couples in more traditional arrangements.

Popularized writing of scientific findings is typically incomplete and seldom reports the methods used in individual studies. There is no greater argument against social change than to claim that what is typical of men and women is an accurate reflection of innate gender capacities. Be cautious about buying into traditional sexual scripts, which are often the basis of popularized advice about sex.

A NOTE ABOUT PORNOGRAPHY

—

Couples therapists often hear women's concern about their husband's use of pornography, while husbands tend to say it's normal and that every guy does it. It's time to look at some recent research to help you decide about how pornography does or does not fit into your marriage.

A 2010 *Scientific American* review of relevant research about pornography (I selected this journal because they tend not to have an agenda about what they present) put forth a few findings I find particularly illuminating:[11]

- ✦ An online study of more than nine thousand people (most of them married men or men in a committed relationship) who used the internet for sexual purposes reported the following results:

- ○ Almost half used porn an hour or less a week.

- ○ 45 percent reported engaging in online sexual activity between one and ten hours a week.

- ○ 8 percent reported engaging in online sexual activity for eleven or more hours a week.

- ○ A small but distinctive 0.5 percent reported engaging in online sexual activity more than seventy hours a week.

- ○ Even relatively light pornography use may have a negative effect on one's partner or spouse.

+ Frequent porn use and enthusiasm for porn was related to male dissatisfaction with a partner's sexual performance and appearance, and doubts about the value of marriage.

+ 42 percent of women in one study said that their partner's porn consumption made them feel insecure, 39 percent that the partner's porn use had a negative effect on their relationship, and 32 percent that it adversely affected their lovemaking.

Is Pornography Adultery?

Ross Douthat, an op-ed writer for *The New York Times*, published an article in 2008 in the *Atlantic*, "Is Pornography Adultery?" His argument is that in hard-core pornography there are actually two sexual acts involved—the on-camera copulation and the masturbation it enables. For Douthat, these are interdependent (neither would happen without the other). His point is that this kind of pornography gets awfully close to moving from "fantasy" sexual activity to "real" sexual activity. If this is real sexual activity with another person, is this not getting close to what we identify as adulterous actions?

Douthat, therefore, challenges the point of view that looking at pornography is a perfectly normal activity, that all men do it, and that women should stop whining and live with it (in part because it is a low-risk alternative to "real" prostitution and "real" affairs).

Douthat, Ross. "Is Pornography Adultery?
The Atlantic. October 2008.

It is informative to read what actual men say about the impact of viewing porn on their sex lives. Here are several descriptions from a 2011 article in *New York Magazine* entitled "He's Just Not That Into Anyone."[12] The men interviewed reported delayed ejaculation, a waning desire for their partners, having to play porno scenes in their mind to orgasm, faking orgasm, "sexual attention deficit disorder" from the habit of jumping quickly from porn clip to porn clip, getting home early from work to masturbate to porn, and thinking their wife didn't measure up to the porn stars, who were younger, hotter, and wilder in the sack.

You would have to be brain-dead to not know that the internet is full of pornography, and that this pornography is viewed predominantly by men. Two elements of modern pornography are: 1) it has greater reach, thanks to the internet, and 2) it has more explicit depictions. This more explicit presentation of sex demonstrates the growing split between "erotic" and "gonzo" porn. Conventional erotic porn mirrors

Hollywood's storytelling style: clear plotlines with both characters and sex serving a romantic end, which typically has a conventional male focus. Gonzo porn is different.

David Rosen describes gonzo porn in an article entitled "Is the Rise of Filthy Gonzo Porn Actually Dangerous, Or Are People Overreacting?"[13] According to Rosen, gonzo porn has pushed the traditional boundaries of pornography to new extremes. This type of porn depicts sexual performances in which a male actor appears to harm the female performer during sex acts that no actual woman would want to engage in. It has no pretensions about plot and characters, sex acts are roughly enacted, with more than one man involved, and the men use explicitly degrading language (women are called sluts, whores, cunts, nasty bitches, etc.) during the performance.

There is reason to be cautious about the potential negative effects on you and your marriage of watching (and masturbating to) pornography—particularly gonzo pornography.

HOW IT WORKS: NEGOTIATING YOUR SEXUAL RELATIONSHIP

—

There is unending advice online and in books about how to communicate about sex. Communication has become such an overused concept that I want to use a different approach here —one more in keeping with the perspective I take about marriage. So, instead of talking about communication here, I'll use the notion of interaction to discuss both how partners should talk to each other about sex and how they can negotiate with one another about sex.

Interacting with your partner in marriage involves two aspects: 1) the content around which the interaction is occurring, and 2) the process that is happening. "Content" refers to the specific issue under discussion—in this case, sex. "Process" refers to what is occurring interpersonally between the two of you as you discuss various aspects of your sexual relationship.

My husband, Joe, does not like to go out to movie theaters. When I approach him about an evening at the movies, I am often skeptical that he will respond favorably, so I am susceptible to being tentative about asking or demanding that we go out, making some complaint about his resistance. (I may be a psychologist, but I am not above interpreting his actions I don't like!) As you can see, my **approach** is not always straightforward, which can increase the likelihood that Joe will react to my **process**—how I am coming across—rather than the actual **content** of the interaction, going to the movie.

Because Joe and I have talked about this difference in what we like to do, he takes the time to be aware of how I am approaching him and not respond to that. He tries to take the time to think about going to the movies: Is he willing to negotiate with me about going or not? Why or why not? On my part, I try to be aware of when I am being tentative or demanding, and then step back from that to focus on what is important to me about going to the movie. How attached am I to seeing this particular movie? Is it about getting out of the house? Is it that I want to be with him at the movie? Am I willing to go on my own or with a friend? These questions are important for me to consider before I make a request, because once I have the answers to them in mind, I can approach Joe in a straightforward manner and negotiate an outcome rather than react to his response.

A lot goes into interacting well with your partner, even about relatively minor content issues like going to a movie. Interaction is always complex and requires self-reflection by both you and your spouse—*especially* when you are talking about sex.

Suppose you are feeling aroused and interested in having sex with your spouse. Like the issue of going to the movie, do you have some preconceived (perhaps stereotypical) idea about how he/she might respond? How will this affect how you approach her/him; are you likely to be tentative or demanding?

Before approaching your partner, think through your interest. Is it mostly about sexual pleasure? Is it about making a connection with your spouse? Is it both? Is it because something is not going well for you and you want comfort through connection? Are you bored? If you think through what exactly your request for sex is about, you will be in a much better position to make your request in a straightforward way. You will also be in a much better position to discuss options for having a sexual encounter that works both for you and your spouse.

If you are the partner responding to the request for sex, pay attention to any automatic response that comes from taking something about the request personally. Think through your interest in sex or the possible interest in sex you could have if you gave it some thought. If both of you come from a position of thoughtful self-reflection about your own wishes and desires for a sexual encounter and how you are approaching your partner, you will be more effective working out together what is sexually satisfying to both of you. The more attention you pay to the way you make your approach, the more satisfying your interactions will be.

One of the ways you can figure out how you generally approach important interactions with your spouse is to think through the defensive or self-protective strategies (outlined in Chapter 3) that you typically use. For example, do you tend to be controlling? Ingratiating? Compliant? If you can identify your preferred protective strategy, be observant about how this affects the way you approach or respond to your spouse in interactions about sex.

With a lot of practice, your interpersonal interactions with your spouse around sexual issues can become quite straightforward. You will automatically:

- ✦ Think through what you want and approach your spouse about sex in a straightforward manner
- ✦ Be equally thoughtful in responding to your spouse's approaches
- ✦ Be open to negotiating an outcome that is satisfying to both of you

SARA AND LUCAS NEGOTIATE

The process of negotiating about sex is the same as the negotiation process I described in Chapter 2. Here is an example of what this sort of negotiation can look like:

Lucas and Sara wanted to discuss how to be better tuned into each other's sexual desires. Sara found that she tended to avoid Lucas's approaches—e.g., his kisses, touches, and snuggles. While she very much enjoyed the physical contact with Lucas, she tended to think that these were preludes to sex, which she wasn't always open to. Lucas, meanwhile, was concerned that Sara was not interested in romantic connections; he was not always thinking about having sexual intercourse when he approached her flirtatiously.

Here are the steps a couple can take to address this issue:

First Step: Approaching Your Partner

When you have something on your mind, give your partner a heads-up about what you want to talk about. It is important to give him/her time to think about his/her own thoughts about the issue. Set a time to talk that is convenient for you both. In this instance, Lucas let Sara know that he was interested in talking about how he approached her romantically. He asked Sara to think through what was important to her about his approach to her. They then set a time on a Saturday morning—about a week after Lucas broached the subject—for their talk, giving Sara some time to think through what her thoughts and wishes were.

Second Step: Expressing What You Want

Until this point in their relationship, Lucas and Sara had not been clear with each other about what they wanted from each other. Nor were they talking to each other about their concerns. When you and your spouse have different perspectives about what is happening in your sex life, your first objective should be to discover the concerns and interests you each have around the specific issue. In an open discussion:

+ Each of you wants to be able to express how you see things.

+ Each of you should be able to clearly explain why what you want is important to you.

+ Each of you should give the other the opportunity to express his/her preference, without interruption.

+ Each of you must watch for hidden personal agendas you may have. If you are feeling anxious or angry, either talk about it or step back and reflect.

When Lucas and Sara had their conversation that Saturday, Lucas talked about his concern that Sara was not interested in him sexually and didn't like closeness with him. Sara told Lucas that she often avoided his flirtations because she thought they would always lead to sexual intercourse but assured him that she was sexually interested in him and did want physical closeness.

Third Step: Recognizing That "Every Concern of Yours Is a Concern of Mine"

Sara and Lucas demonstrated that "every concern of yours is a concern of mine" through this open discussion. Rather than simply defending their own position, they listened to each other and honored what the other thought was important. Being able to be clear about your specific concerns in each situation and being able to clearly state this concern is important to finding workable solutions to the issue or disagreement.

Final Step: Make a Plan That Works for Both of You

The best outcome of this kind of discussion is a win-win action plan that is responsive to the stated concerns. Here is what Lucas and Sara decided on: Going forward, Lucas would be clear and direct about when he wished to have sexual intercourse with Sara; he would signal his intention as he began his approach. They agreed that he would say something like, "Would you like to meet in the bedroom tonight?" in a playful manner if his intention was to approach her for sexual intercourse. Sara, in turn, could be openly responsive to his playful romantic teasing and touching without hesitation because she would know what to expect. When Lucas did signal that he was interest in sexual intercourse, Sara would consider her own interest and/or her openness to being available for sexual intercourse, and then respond appropriately.

BE PROACTIVE IN NEGOTIATING YOUR SEXUAL RELATIONSHIP

―――

You will want to be proactive in your discussions about how to create a satisfying sexual relationship. Having ongoing discussions about sexual issues (which is a good idea!) requires considerable self-reflection. It also means you are going to negotiate *all* the issues you and your spouse raise in these discussions; that's the only way to ensure that you're creating the sexually satisfying relationship you both want.

Here are some ideas of things to talk about:

+ How you learned about sex
+ In what way is sex important to you
+ Whether either of you has had a traumatic sexual experience
+ What fears you have about your body
+ How often you would like to have some kind of sex
+ How sexual acts will be performed
+ Which sexual acts you would enjoy
+ Whether either or both of you watch pornography
+ Anything else you can think of that is likely to have an impact on your sexual relations specifically, and on the overall quality of your marriage

Here is a chart you can use as a way of opening discussion between you and your spouse about sexual issues. Make a sheet for each of you; fill in what you think and how you feel about each of the issues listed as well as others you would like to discuss. Set a time to share with each other your individual perspectives. Follow the process described above as a guide for your discussions and negotiations.

Issue	What do you think?	What does your partner think?	Can we create a win-win approach?
Initiating sex			
Asking for a specific sex act			
How I learned about sex			
Deciding about pornography			
What fears have you about sex?			

There is no reason to think that you cannot communicate collaboratively about your sex life in the same way that you communicate about anything of real value in your marriage.

CHAPTER 5 ——————

TAKEAWAYS

Acknowledge the tension that exists in every relationship between the safety and security you get from being married and the excitement you feel in being separate people with independent interests.

Don't get bogged down in sexual stereotypes about how *men* and *women* approach sex; you are individual people.

Remember to keep "fresh eyes" about your spouse; remember how you valued and adored him/her when you first met.

Be cautious about if and how pornography plays out in your marriage.

Pay attention to how your personal insecurities can play out in your sexual relationship.

Good sex is about feelings more than functioning.

Remember to express your sexual desires through your sexual preference. Do not elevate these sexual preferences to sexual needs.

Learn to interact collaboratively about sex the same way you do about anything important to you in your marriage.

Communicating well will allow you to negotiate with your spouse to achieve a satisfying and sustainable sexual relationship in your marriage.

6

The Unexamined Male Libido

This chapter is about how you, as a husband, can become more self-reflective about your sexual desire or libido, which can be a boon to your marital relationship—or a hindrance to it. Stephen Marche, a Canadian journalist and author who writes about culture, penned an article for *The New York Times* in November 2017 titled "The Unexamined Brutality of the Male Libido."[1] In the article, he challenges men to examine their own ideas about male sexual desire or libido in the context of increasing equality between men and women.

The sexual harassment scandals that have surfaced in recent years make the need for this self-assessment more evident. These accusations, which have been made against many different kinds of men, have exposed the reality of the lived experience of women. Marche claims that male sexuality in the context of the inequality of a patriarchal society can be brutal. He believes that the pathologies of masculine libido exposed in these sexual harassment scandals typically go unexamined by men themselves. In fact, Marche thinks men's sexual desire, in general, has gone unexamined by men. Men, however—who typically receive no education about sex besides high school sex courses and traditional masculine scripts that do not promote self-reflection—are woefully unprepared for this kind of self-evaluation.

This chapter is designed to stimulate your own thinking about your masculinity, how this relates to your sexual desire, and how this plays out in your marriage.

MALE SEXUAL DESIRE COOPTED BY OUTDATED IDEAS OF MASCULINITY

Since the feminist revolution of the 1970s, traditional ideas of masculinity (maintained during what Marche calls "the hollow patriarchy") have been under challenge. To the degree that the hollow patriarchy still holds, men are still expected to be powerful but are increasingly losing the authority that has traditionally supported that power.

Some men have felt the double whammy of loss of economic status (as jobs in traditionally masculine sectors have disappeared) and loss of social status (as women have advanced economically and socially).[2] Two significant factors have contributed to this economic and social shift for men: First, women have been succeeding in the classroom; girls have overtaken boys at every stage of education, not because of superior intellect but because of greater focus, effort, and self-discipline. Boys are more likely to be distracted by video games or derailed by drink or drugs. Women have advanced steadily in the workplace because they have a better education and more skills. Second, the labor market is becoming more female friendly. Women have moved into formerly all-male areas like law, medicine, and business, while men largely have not moved into the areas that have typically been female dominated. Most of the jobs that have been created since the Great Recession of 2008 have been in the so-called HEAL areas of health, education, administration, and literacy—and men have not been taking these new jobs. The real obstacle to men becoming schoolteachers or nurses is cultural and attitudinal, of course; it has nothing to do with the nature of the job. It is important for men to start thinking about acquiring skills in the HEAL jobs that have been traditionally held by women and so are defined as feminine. These are the jobs of the future that are replacing the so-called masculine jobs in manufacturing.

Too many of the young men displaced by these changes are trying to hold out for a traditional marriage—an archetype that has largely disappeared—or deciding not to marry at all. A refuge for some of these displaced men has been hyper-masculinity, an attitude they adopt in compensation for the jobs they think have been taken away from them. This hyper-masculinity can devolve into racism, neo-Nazism, and explicit misogyny.

Marche notes that many men have become confused, self pitying, melancholy, guilty feeling, and vulnerable because of these economic and social changes. Gone are the traditionally defined go-it-alone, take-charge, lonely, heroic icons: the cowboy, the astronaut, even the gangster. In popular culture, Marche notes, the stock male character of all contemporary comedies is now the man-boy who wants to drink beer rather than talk to his wife or take care of his kids. The man cave is the perfect exemplar of masculinity that does not have actual power but is still perceived as an icon of power. Here, men recover their manliness only by hiding from the world.

There is also increasing demand being placed on men for greater involvement in the home, which challenges the traditional breadwinner role of the male provider. No longer are most women content with being the homemaker wife who unstintingly supports her husband's place in the work world. In her book *Stiffed: The Betrayal of the American Man*, Susan Faludi argues that many men have "lost their compass in the world" because of the cultural changes that have occurred in America. She says we have moved from being a traditional society that valued loyalty, team play, and vocational mastery to an "ornamental culture."[3] This "ornamental culture" is one in which competitive individualism is not tied to a domain of work but is ruled by commercial values—values that are defined by who has the most, the best, the biggest, the fastest. The old formula for attaining manhood has vanished . . . in short order.

FROM PATRIARCHY TO PATERNITY LEAVE: MASCULINITY IN AN EQUITABLE MARRIAGE

Marche argues that masculinity and the male libido still go largely unexamined by men themselves.[4] Yet I would say that there seems to be a growing interest by men today, in response to the changing culture, in how to reimagine their own sense of masculinity. There do, however, continue to be proponents of a throwback masculinity—men who are trying to reclaim traditional models of maleness. One such proponent, pointed out by Marche, is Harvey Mansfield, a Harvard government professor, who uses the term "retrosexual" to describe affluent urban men who wear hunting garb, buy designer axes, and write about the art of manliness on blogs.

Andrew Romano, a journalist at *Newsweek*, argues that men should not try to stick to some musty script of masculinity.[5] The notion of masculinity, he says, needs to be broadened to include both "Mr. T and Mr. Mom." Romano pleads that we must reimagine what men do both at home and at work, thereby expanding the notion of manhood. He thinks, as I do, that the place to start is in the home. Buying into an equitable marriage, negotiating all that encompasses (household tasks, child rearing, and sex) may be what is needed not only to keep the American male alive and well, as Romano argues, but to keep America itself competitive in the twenty-first century.

On the surface, the New Macho is a paradox, a path to masculinity paved with girly jobs and dirty diapers. Dig a little deeper, however, and it begins to make a lot of sense—not just for men but for everyone. If men embraced parental leave, women would be spared the stigma of the "mommy track"—and the professional penalties (like lower pay) that come along with it. If men were more involved fathers, more kids might stay in school, steer clear of crime, and avoid poverty as adults. And if the country achieved gender parity in the workplace—an optimal balance of fully employed men and women—the gross domestic product would grow by as much as 9 percent, according to a recent study by the World Economic Forum.

Ultimately, the New Macho boils down to a simple principle: In a changing world, men should do whatever it takes to contribute their fair share at home and at work. And after all, what's more masculine: being a strong, silent, unemployed, absentee father, or fulfilling your half of the bargain as a breadwinner and a dad?[6]

SEXUAL DESIRE IN AN EQUITABLE RELATIONSHIP

In "The Unexamined Brutality of the Male Libido," Marche talks about male libido (i.e., male sexual desire) as "often ugly and dangerous." He also posits that this "often ugly and dangerous" male sexual desire may be an impediment to the reconciliation between gender equality and human desire. He asks the question, "How are we supposed to create an equal world when male mechanisms of desire are inherently brutal?" As you might imagine, Marche got a lot of blowback for these ideas. The general reaction was that while outdated ideas of masculinity can result in the kind of brutality described in the current sexual harassment stories, male sexual desire is not *inherently* brutal.

I am not exactly sure what Marche means by "brutal" sexual desire. I suspect he is falling back on some popular myths about male sexual desire—that men, for example, feel strong (almost uncontrollable) urges to have intercourse and to masturbate, are willing to take sexual risks regardless of the consequences, don't care about love and just want to get laid, have a perpetually high sex drive, etc.

It is incumbent on you to get beyond stereotypical, gendered views of your sexual desire. The findings from some recent research by Sari van Anders, a behavioral neuroendocrinologist at the University of Michigan, may help.[7] She solicited 196 (105 men and 91 women) college students and community volunteers to complete questionnaires about their sex lives (sexual desire with a partner and sexual desire for masturbation), their stress (measured by cortisol), and their body image. They answered questions about how frequently they had partnered sex and masturbated, and how frequently they had the desire to masturbate or to have sex with a partner. The subjects also provided saliva for testing levels of cortisol (a stress hormone) and testosterone.

One of the important aspects of this study is looking at sexual desire both as a solo experience (masturbation) and as sexual desire for a partner. Van Anders hypothesized that the desire to have sex with someone may be different from the desire to masturbate. The desire to masturbate may be a purer measure of what we think of as sexual desire. The desire for sex with another person may be influenced by other sociocultural and interpersonal factors, e.g., how you felt about your partner that day, how attracted you are to your partner, and your overall relationship quality.

Interestingly, even surprisingly, van Anders found that when she compared low- versus high-testosterone participants and their self-reported levels of desire, levels of testosterone were not related to how much the men thought about either solitary sex or partnered sex.

Boy, does this finding fly in the face of the idea that men's sexual desire is driven by testosterone. What typically is found in animal studies and studies of men who produce extremely low levels of testosterone is that men generally desire sex (not distinguishing between solo sex and partnered sex) more frequently than women *and* that men also produce more testosterone than women. These two independent findings led to belief that testosterone is the reason for desire. Van Anders, however, argues that the typical healthy range of testosterone found in men is high enough (even for the men in the low-testosterone group) that changes in testosterone are not enough to account for changes in sexual desire.

The one thing van Anders found that seems to fit the stereotype about men and women is that men masturbated more than women and reported more sexual desire (with a partner or solo). Women in the study reported less masturbation and less desire. For van Anders this raises the question of which comes first, the desire for or the actual masturbation? Perhaps masturbation affects sexual desire, which then accounts for the difference between men's and women's reported sexual desire.

Earlier I talked about how prevalent the idea is that in marriage you must fulfill each other's needs. Remember, the idea that we have sexual needs is so prevalent that it has become psychological dogma. Van Anders's research supports the idea that sexual desire for your spouse is influenced by social and psychological factors as well as by the hormone testosterone. I believe this strongly supports my own position—that sex in marriage between husband and wife must be negotiated collaboratively. Sexual desire must be honored, yes, but it cannot justify a demand that requires fulfillment independent of negotiation between consenting partners. Your sexual desire is occurring in the context of partnered sex, and this means old ideas must give way to negotiating collaboratively regarding your sexual relationship.

CHAPTER 6 —————————

T
A It is important to be self-reflective about
your own sense of masculinity.

K
E Your sexual desire can be a boon to your
A relationship, as long as it's not driven by a
distorted sense of masculinity.

W
A Testosterone is not a metaphor for—cannot
stand for—masculinity.

Y
S Being masculine needs to include both being
Mr. Mom and Mr. Executive.

Sexual desire for your partner is not the same
thing as the desire to masturbate.

Your sexual relationship with your partner is
influenced by social and psychological
factors.

7

Choosing Fidelity

Marital fidelity is typically assumed to be agreed upon once you take your marriage vows at the wedding, and sexual fidelity is codified (arranged by laws or rules into a systematic code) in most religions. However, I do not believe you can rely either on personal assumptions or systematic codes to ensure faithfulness in your marriage. Here are some recent statistics on infidelity from the Statistic Brain Research Institute:[1]

Percent men admitting to infidelity in any relationship	57%
Percent women admitting to infidelity in any relationship	54%
Percent married men who strayed at least once during marriage	22%
Percent married women who strayed at least once during marriage	14%
Percent men & women admitting to having affair with co-worker	36%
Percent men & women admitting to infidelity on business trips	35%
Average length of affair	2 years
Percent men who would have affair if knew would not get caught	74%
Percent women who would have affair if knew would not get caught	68%

Between these statistics and my own experience working with couples, I'm convinced that we should all be changing the way we think about fidelity in marriage. This new approach to fidelity in marriage, which has been called the "new monogamy," requires that you negotiate explicitly and collaboratively what fidelity means in your marriage in the same way you should be negotiating all the important aspects of your relationship. This approach means that you understand that monogamy is not a given but rather a choice you and your spouse are making together. It also means that monogamy is negotiated collaboratively not only at the beginning and of your marital relationship but also on an ongoing basis.

Before I offer some ideas about the issues you will want to think about in creating a "new monogamy" in your own marriage, I want to review how society supports infidelity and the psychology of the "old monogamy"—i.e., the idea that fidelity is an implicit commitment we all make when we enter into marriage.

HOW SOCIETY SUPPORTS INFIDELITY

———

Peggy Vaughan, author of *The Monogamy Myth*, promotes the idea that monogamy is a myth that is inconsistent with what really happens in relationships in our society.[2] Vaughan uses the term "monogamy myth" to challenge the widely held belief that monogamy is the norm that is supported by society. She argues that society contributes to infidelity by encouraging a **code of secrecy** about sex and affairs, which indirectly enables us to engage in affairs—and I agree. So, before you attempt to negotiate a new monogamy for your own marriage, I encourage you to look at the ways in which our society implicitly sanctions, encourages, and/or supports affairs.

First, we learn early in life that it is okay to lie about sex. We do that as teenagers, keeping our first sexual adventures secret from our parents. This leads us to believe that secrecy about our affairs is appropriate and required. There's an old admonition that if you are challenged about an affair, "Never tell; if questioned, deny it." This is the code of secrecy in operation.

Second, the more stereotypically we view our roles in marriage, the more vulnerable we are to affairs, where we can "be ourselves" and have fun, variety, and freedom. We may be looking for that ideal person who will make us feel happy and fulfilled.

Our society's treatment of women as sex objects—especially in advertising, which sells the idea of women as one of the many good things that a man deserves—also contributes to the likelihood of both men and women having affairs. In a man's view, an affair is something he deserves; for women, it is a validation of their attractiveness.

Third, we can find a subtle kind of support for affairs from friends, in the sense that it can be exciting to tell our friends of our taboo dalliances. This may be particularly true for men, who are more likely than women to get satisfaction from impressing their friends with stories of their adventures.

Fourth, professional support for secrecy can come from marriage counselors and advice columnists, many of whom are adamant that a person having an affair should not tell his/her partner about the affair. This advice fails to consider the risks associated with not being honest with one's spouse, particularly if the marriage is to continue.

A key part of negotiating a new monogamy is that there can be no secrecy between you and your spouse about the arrangements you arrive at through your negotiation of monogamy in your marriage.

THE PSYCHOLOGY OF THE "OLD MONOGAMY"

Esther Perel, whom you met in Chapter 5, turns to psychoanalytic and relational theories to examine the basis for our profound belief in the old monogamy.[3] This perspective suggests that monogamy has its psychological roots in our early experiences.

As children, our experience with our primary caretakers is (hopefully) one in which love is unconditionally and wholeheartedly given, without us having to make any effort to win that love. Early experience is one of oneness with the other; there is no distinction for the baby between him/herself and mother. It's the ultimate togetherness. Of course, what is true is that mother knows and cares about many other people, including what the child experiences as a "jealous" father. So, as Perel notes, mother was never totally faithful, not even once upon a time.

I believe this analysis is significant in understanding what Perel calls "monolithic monogamy," which is the ultimate seeking of exclusiveness with another person. This is the idea that there is one person out there who can be everything you want: confidant, best friend, and passionate lover. The old monogamy is the sacred cow of this romantic ideal because it is the marker for our own specialness. This is the specialness that deserves exclusiveness, and it's what leads us to get lost in a sense of personal betrayal and rejection when infidelity occurs.

Negotiating a new monogamy is enhanced by the understanding that the convention of old monogamy is based on our early longing for this specialness. Better to negotiate and renegotiate fidelity as a measure of the commitment to your relationship rather than try to fulfill your wish for specialness through your spouse.

MY TAKE ON THE EFFECTS OF INFIDELITY

Infidelity in marriage is a difficult thing to deal with for everyone. From my experience in working with couples in which one partner has had an affair, the first issue is always the pain the person who has been cheated on feels. There is a personal sense of betrayal, the feeling of being personally rejected. But *what* is betrayed; *what* is rejected?

I am going to take a controversial position: **I believe the betrayal and rejection is of the relationship, not the person.**

Before you close the book, let me explain. For me, adultery is a betrayal of the connection (the relationship) between you and your spouse. What you thought about the relationship is not true. **Your understanding of the relationship is not true.** Your partner has disinvested him/herself in the relationship and hasn't told you this. For me, this is the betrayal—the fact that your spouse has rejected your relationship and not been truthful about that rejection.

A better way to understand the individual impact of adultery is to assess the **personal harm** that this relationship betrayal causes you. From my perspective, the two greatest harms caused by adultery are: 1) being kept in the dark through secrecy, and 2) the loss of the connection with someone you love. The **secrecy** of the affair prevents you from making informed decisions about your own welfare; the entire time the affair is occurring you are making hundreds of decisions about the things in life that matter to you without having all the information you need in hand.

The great personal loss of the connection you thought you had with your spouse can be disorienting, threatening, and seemingly unendurable.

The harm done to the adulterer is that he/she is being dishonest in a most intimate way in the marriage. He/she has disinvested him/herself in the relationship without informing you. Being dishonest in this fundamental way affects a person's very character.

Viewing infidelity in this way drove me to find a better way to maintain fidelity in marriage. The way of thinking about fidelity that I've found fits best with my perspective on marriage is that it must be a matter of **conviction rather**

than convention. And this conviction to maintain fidelity in your marriage can be accomplished by using the principles set out in this book on how to achieve an equitable and sustainable marriage through collaborative negotiation.

Rather than seeking specialness in your relationship, understand that you and your spouse are **unique** people who are committed to an equitable and sustainable marriage through the process of negotiation. The specialness is in the relationship, not in you as an individual.

FIDELITY AS CONVICTION

The best approach you can take as you begin your marriage is to adopt Parel's position that fidelity is a matter of **conviction rather than convention.** As noted above, this means you understand that monogamy is no longer a societal given, need not be driven by subconscious wishes, and is best seen as a choice you two are making together. It means that monogamy can be a negotiated decision. Discussing and negotiating monogamy in your relationship directly challenges outdated ideas about monogamy and the "code of secrecy" about sex and infidelity.

Both you and your spouse must take the time to reflect on your own thoughts and feelings about sexual fidelity in your marriage. Examine your *implicit* view of monogamy. This is likely to be influenced by your own family background, religious beliefs, traditional sex roles, personal moral values, and personal insecurities. The two of you are likely to have a different understanding of the implicit agreement of the old monogamy. Such implicit ideas may include:[4]

+ "We promise to be faithful until one of us grows tired of the other."

+ "I know you won't cheat, but I probably will."

+ "I'll be faithful, but you won't because you're a guy."

+ "We'll be faithful except for a little swinging when we go on vacation."

You must make these implicit ideas explicit. These implicit views are what you need to talk about with your spouse.

Once you and your spouse establish guidelines for maintaining your monogamous relationship, your job is to continually revisit them. These guidelines can be renegotiated over the course of your marriage, particularly at times of transition—e.g., when you have children, when you have career changes, when you retire, as you age.

There are three important things to consider about creating a new monogamy: honesty/openness, the outside relationship, and sexual fidelity.[5] Being **honest** and **open** refers to what you agree to tell each other about your relationships with other people. This can include mentioning that you are attracted to and/or have fantasies about another person. The **outside relationship** refers to deciding on the limits on the nature of your relationships with other people. Is it okay to share personal information and intimate thoughts with others, to meet colleagues for dinner, etc.? And finally, what does

sexual fidelity mean to the two of you? What about lusting after someone, pornography use, and emotional and/or sexual relationships that happen on the internet?

We are living longer these days, which means that many of us can expect (or at least hope) to stay sexually and emotionally connected to our spouses for forty or more years. If you want to cocreate an equitable marriage with your partner that can last over the long haul, fidelity must be a conscious choice you make. Ultimately, this will make for better parenting and encourage the emotional creativity you'll both need in order to get along for that many years. This requires the relational competencies outlined in this book, including self-awareness, cultural awareness, conscious empathy, and kindness.

Negotiate fidelity regularly with your spouse; in doing so, you will protect your most intimate bond while continuing to grow as individuals.

MY ADVICE TO YOU

——

Do not ever hesitate to seek guidance from a professional regarding: negotiating about sex, negotiating about fidelity, and negotiating about infidelity. Choose a professional who helps build your confidence about negotiating sexual issues. Most professionals have their own approach to sexuality and ideas about fidelity. Ask the person you're considering seeing about their approach. If after working with them, you do not feel comfortable, seek out someone else.

CHAPTER 7 ————————————

T
A
K
E
A
W
A
Y
S

Begin your marriage by becoming smarter about what it means to be sexually faithful to each other.

Make fidelity a choice the two of you can negotiate.

Myths about monogamy and a "code of silence" about fidelity may encourage and/or support infidelity.

Infidelity is a betrayal and rejection of the marriage relationship, not you personally.

You may need help in both assessing and working through the harm done to you by infidelity if it occurs.

You can survive infidelity in your marriage if it happens; it will, however, take a lot of work.

Fidelity is a matter of conviction rather than convention.

PART IV

———

THE REVOLUTION
AT WORK

8

Balancing Family
and Work

Now that you have an idea of how to work on yourself and
your relationship, it is time to talk about how this translates
into the two of you taking on the world of work—a world
that is still unfriendly to families, a world that must evolve.

You will have significant choices to make about what you
want from your marriage, your family, and your work. A huge
issue is how to manage household tasks and childcare in the
context of your work situations. Fortunately, couples who
have successfully managed this difficult task have good ideas
they can share with you.

In this chapter, I suggest you review what kind of marriage you want to have. Richard Reeves has some ideas about
this. I will also talk about the "fair" division of household responsibilities and how resistance to sharing responsibility can
play out in your relationship, and then end with a review of
an important research project that asked couples who were
successfully balancing family and work how they did it.

THINK ABOUT WHAT KIND
OF MARRIAGE YOU WANT

———

This is the time to consider what kind of marriage you want to have. Therapist Susan Pease Gadoua and journalist Vicki Larson tell us that we have more latitude today in defining a marriage that suits our own life plans than couples have in the past.[1] In their book *The New I Do*, they talk about the different ways in which couples can say "I Do"—e.g., starter marriage, companionship marriage, parenting marriage, and covenant marriage, among others—and the pros and cons of each. Gadoua and Larson do a nice job of tracing the history of marriage, showing that what we consider "traditional marriage" is actually a relatively recent form.

Richard Reeves of the Brookings Institute says that while there are now many forms of marriage like those described by Gadoua and Larson, we can still identify three key reasons people get married that seem to define three different kinds of marriages: traditional, romantic, and parental.[2] The **traditional marriage** is defined by gender roles, where the husband is the breadwinner and the wife is the homemaker. As Reeves says, "Husbands bring home the bacon. Wives cook it." These are the kinds of marriages that the world of work has created. These marriages are often supported by religious faith, duty, and faithfulness between husband and wife, with an emphasis on the children in the family. (Gadoua and Larson argue that we have been outgrowing this kind of marriage since the 1960s.)

The **romantic marriage** is a marriage based on the idea of self-actualization through the intimate relationship between husband and wife. In romantic marriages, the focus is on the adult relationship, not the parent-child relationship. As Reeves says, "Romantic marriages are passionate, stimulating, and sexy." Parenting, by contrast, involves hard physical labor, repetitive tasks, and exhaustion. Gadoua and Larson note that the 1970s "me generation" gave rise to the idea of choosing a soul mate as a basis for creating the romantic marriage. They also note that this era saw the rise of marriage enrichment programs that promoted traditional gender roles, probably as a backlash to the rising divorce rate and the women's movement.

The 1980s saw an increase in the number of people never marrying. There was also a significant increase in couples divorcing. During this period, more women began working outside the home, and women's careers became less subordinate to men's. These and other significant cultural changes continued to evolve throughout the 1990s—despite efforts by many traditionalists to maintain the status quo.

Reeves defines the **HIP (high-investment parenting) marriage** as one that is liberal about adult roles and conservative about raising children. A basic goal for this type of marriage is to raise children together in a settled, nurturing environment, while striving to create and maintain a loving marital relationship. In this type of marriage, the wife is not economically dependent on her husband. HIP wives typically have a good education and want to have a career outside the home with high earning potential. As Gerson's study noted, these marriages will not survive unless these women are supported in their economic independence.

IS THE HIP MARRIAGE FOR YOU?

——

Couples trying to create a HIP marriage strive for a marital relationship that supports balance by: sharing housework, having equal financial influence, both partners valuing one another's work and life goals, sharing the emotional work of the family, and both partners showing active involvement in taking care of the children.

High-investment parenting is about a huge commitment of time, energy, money, and attention to all aspects of your children's care and development. Because of the significant change in women's economic and social status in recent decades, HIP marriages are recasting family responsibilities, with couples sharing the roles of both child raiser and moneymaker.

HIP couples also want to create and maintain a vibrant, loving relationship. This type of marriage takes the commitment of self-awareness and of willingness to negotiate collaboratively with each other. This is the type of marriage I have discussed throughout this book.

THE COMMITMENT TO FAMILY AND WORK

——

Young people today tend to have liberal ideas about adult roles, including strongly rejecting differentiated gender roles in marriage. However, a recent study of Harvard Business School alumni found that the real lives of Harvard women graduates did not match their reported expectations about their work and family lives.[3] That is, while women and men have about equal expectations about how their careers and home life will go, the actual lives of the women in the study did not live up to those expectations.

For example, young women surveyed in this study expected that their progressive values about caring for children would be reflected in their own lives. However, like the men and women in Gerson's book *The Unfinished Revolution*, the young men in the Harvard study were much more likely to expect a more traditional outcome—i.e., that the women they married would be more responsible for caring for children.

Here are a few of the findings from this study of Harvard Business School alumni:

+ Male and female graduates have the same goals: Meaningful, satisfying work (with opportunities for career growth), and fulfilling personal lives.

+ Among full-time workers, men were significantly more likely to be in senior management positions.

+ Fewer women than men reported being satisfied with careers.

+ Different expectations in marriage lead to diverging career paths.

+ Seventy-five percent of men (ages thirty-two to sixty-seven) expected their careers to take precedence over their wives' careers, and that turned out to be true.

+ Half of corresponding women expected to handle the majority of childcare in their household; three-fourths ended up doing so.

What is interesting about this study is that it asked the survey takers to report on the **gender dynamics** (how they interacted with each other) of their own lives, not about gender equality in the abstract. These are bright, well-educated women and men who, once they marry and have children, fell back into traditional roles.

How does this happen? Very subtly!

You will be **"doing gender"** daily in your marriage without even knowing it.[4] Image a husband who has had a hard day at work and is feeling stressed. He "acts out" his gender expectations by crumpling into his easy chair to show that he is worn out from work and needs some attention. His wife, seeing this, intuitively understands that this is his bid for her to show her "womanly" caring. How she responds depends on her definition of being feminine. She may respond by sitting down with him for a few minutes, or by bringing him something to eat or drink. She may not ask him to talk about his day because this is not the kind of attention he prefers. For her not to provide the expected caring would likely result in him feeling deprived of what he is due. (See the box "Doing Gender," which describes where this term comes from.)

"Doing Gender"

"Doing Gender," a concept introduced by Candace West and Don Zimmerman in the late '80s, refers to the idea that gender, rather than being primarily an innate quality of individuals, is how we come to perceive ourselves through our everyday interactions with each other. In other words, we construct the idea of masculinity and femininity by the way we as men and women interact with each other.

The concept of doing gender was inspired by the social psychologist Erving Goffman, who argued that we believe that each of us has an essential nature that is expressed in our actions. One of the most basic essential natures about people is one's masculinity and femininity. So, when we see men and women behaving in specific ways in interaction with one another, we assume it is because of innate gender differences in masculinity and femininity.

An alternative way of thinking about doing gender is that we act according to scripts. Scripts are culturally based assumptions about this essential nature idea of men and women and what it means to be masculine and feminine. Doing gender using scripts means adjusting our actions to make them consistent with how a specific culture's society expects men and women to act.

Candace West and Don Zimmerman. "Doing Gender," *Gender and Society* 1, no. 2 (1987).

The husband and wife in this ordinary interaction are defining themselves as masculine and feminine by confirming each other's gendered expectations of being a caring wife and husband. It is noteworthy that conforming to these gender roles is not necessarily seen as praiseworthy—it is what *ought to be done.*

In contrast, let's see what a de-gendered interaction might look like. Our husband has had a tough day at work, and his wife, who is on family leave from her work, is home with their newborn. He guesses that she, too, may have had a tough day with their colicky baby. After greeting her and confirming that, indeed, she has had a tough day, he suggests they call his mother to come over for a couple of hours so they can have dinner out. At dinner, both have a chance to share about their difficult day, each supporting the other. They also continue the conversation about how they are going to arrange their work life to accommodate their new, loved member of the family.

The first scenario is of a couple automatically doing gender—i.e., enacting traditional gender roles subconsciously. When we do gender, we are being kind, helpful, doing the thing that is expected of us as wives or husbands. For example, a husband is described as helping his wife with *her* household tasks; he babysits regularly; her leisure time is spent in family activities, while his leisure time is for himself; she is responsible for the emotional well-being of the family, while he is responsible for the economic well-being of the family. Accepting these gender prescriptions perpetuates old ideas about what it means to be a masculine husband and a feminine wife in your marriage. Subtly reinforcing gender-differentiated roles for you and your spouse in your marriage creates your own private gender factory.

One of the biggest decisions you will make in your marriage is whether one or both of you will work outside the home, and what the characteristics of those jobs will be. Many factors will affect this decision. What are your financial and career goals? How much gratification do you get from work? How are your energy levels? How much time do you want to devote to caring for your children? These are life-altering decisions you make that require all the self-awareness you can muster and all the collaborative negotiating skills you have learned.

OBSESSING OVER A FAIR DIVISION
OF LABOR

Couples can find advice from many sources on how to split housework to create equality. Much of this advice relies too heavily on being fair, which requires an objective evaluation of who does what. Trying to be objective about doing tasks propels you into a tit-for-tat or exchange approach to housework—like it's a business transaction—and this doesn't work in marriage because exchange transactions are based on maximizing one's self-interest, not about tending to your relationship.

Noah Berlatsky, an author and editor who writes about comics, science fiction, and pop culture, advises couples to avoid splitting household tasks evenly because marriage is not about the obligations that result from a quid-pro-quo, businesslike transaction.[5] Rather, it's about caring for and about each other. Berlatsky says that he and his wife sometimes split tasks they both dislike; sometimes they make a pact of laziness, agreeing to not do specific tasks. They order out a lot because neither likes to cook much.

In an article titled "The Case for Filth," Stephen Marche suggests we do less and care less about tidiness: don't make the beds, don't repaint the peeling ceilings, outsource whatever household tasks you can, etc.[6] In my sidebar here on "The Case for Filth," I describe how housework can be divided between well-educated, egalitarian husbands and wives who fall back on gender scripts. Marriages can slide toward a gender-driven hierarchy if you are not careful about how you negotiate household activities. As Berlatsky says, many years of inequity and a lot of learned gender obligation can end up feeling like, and even functioning like, slavery. The goal in managing your household, Berlatsky says, "is not to clear your ledger, but to live with each other, and love each other, day in and day out for the rest of your lives."

The Case for Filth

The "Case for Filth" is the fun title of a *NYT* opinion piece by Stephen Marche about a 2015 study of patterns of housework as determined by gender and parenthood. The study found that:

- Gender is what determines who does housework and childcare even though more mothers today work and both men and women said they wanted to share.
- Men and women's share of housework is more similar today than it was in the '60s because of a steep reduction in women's housework and modest increase in men's housework.
- Both men and women spend more time with their children today than they did in the past.

Some suggestions Marche makes about household management:

- Don't let housework be a feminist issue; it is not something wives owe to their husbands.
- Housework and childcare are the stuff relationships are made of; it's about helping each other.

Steve Marche. "The Case for Filth." *New York Times.* December 21, 2013.

RESISTANCE SHOWS UP

———

Why is it so hard to figure out household chores in an egalitarian relationship? Here are a few thoughts about the way in which you can resist the gender-driven division of labor that you have inherited.

The Household Is Women's Traditional Sphere of Influence and Expertise. Remember, being feminine gets tied to managing the household, even for committed couples in which both partners work. Husbands' sense of masculinity may get tied to viewing their participation as helping out or taking on chores on an ad hoc basis.

Women Can Inadvertently Discourage Husbands from Doing Their Share. Wives can be critical of the way in which husbands do household tasks; husbands need to empower themselves at home.

Most of Us Believe We Are Doing Nearly All of the Work. Psychologists see this as a trick of overclaiming. Overclaiming is an example of how self-centered most of us are. You can recall the times *you* cleaned the kitchen more easily than you can remember the times your partner did. It is also the case that we fail to appreciate the effort put forth in doing such tasks. Whatever task I am doing, I am aware not only of the actual work done, I am intimately aware of the effort it takes me to do the job. I don't experience my spouse's effort. Effort is perceptual, not objective.

A study of the nearly two hundred highly educated couples in Ohio State University's New Parents Project longitudinal study wanted and had egalitarian marriages.[7] In-depth time diaries showed that both the men and women, on average, worked about forty hours. **Then they had a baby.** When the babies were nine months old, after whatever parental leave either parent took, time diary data showed that the women continued to do about fifteen hours a week of housework, and they **added** twenty-two hours a week of childcare. The men picked up fourteen hours more of childcare, but they started doing **less** housework—an average of five **fewer** hours a week. (More about sharing parenting in Chapter 9.)

SUCCESSFUL COUPLES WORK AT IT

Researchers at Colorado State University studied forty-seven middle-class, dual-earner couples with children to identify key strategies for how to successfully balance family and work. Here are the ten strategies that these couples found were vital in maintaining family-work balance in an equal relationship.[8] These are the kinds of choices successful couples make to achieve the kind of marriage they want, described in their own words:

1. **Valuing Family.** Successful couples stress the importance of keeping family as their highest priority. They proactively create opportunities for family time,

such as pizza night on Friday or bedtime stories every night. It is not uncommon for these couples to limit their work hours, sacrifice career advancement, make career changes, or accept less prestigious positions to keep family as their number one priority.

2. **Striving for Partnership.** Couples reported that striving for equality in their relationship by being partners was critical to their success. Three important parts of this striving were: being sure that the household tasks were "our" responsibility not "hers" or "his"; making decisions together as partners; and being partners on an interpersonal level in an effort to develop greater respect, appreciation, and support for one another.

3. **Deriving Meaning from Work.** Successful couples experience enjoyment of and a sense of purpose in their careers and jobs, which brings energy and enthusiasm to their lives, as well as ensures their family's well-being. This energy and enthusiasm limits work-related fatigue and burnout.

4. **Maintaining Work Boundaries.** Successful couples make a commitment to maintain control over work, not allowing careers to dictate the pace of their lives. They consciously and purposely separate family and work. They make a conscious effort to set limits on work, creating clear boundaries for their professional commitments (this requires negotiating with employers).

5. **Focusing and Producing at Work.** Being productive at work is important to successful couples. Setting limits on their careers has not adversely affected their productivity. When they're at work, they don't mess around. This productivity is key to their employer's support of their efforts to manage family and work even as they set the boundaries they desire.

6. **Prioritizing Family Fun.** Successful couples use play and family fun as a way of relaxing, enjoying life, staying emotionally connected, and creating balance in their lives. The study couples also said that having a sense of humor—being able to laugh at life—was important in keeping life enjoyable and balanced.

7. **Taking Pride in Dual Earning.** These couples believe dual earning is positive for all members of their family and do not accept the negative societal message about their family arrangement. The couples in this study tended not to struggle with feelings of guilt about not spending every minute of their day engaged in quality time with their children. They felt they had a good balance of playing with their children, working, attending to household chores, and spending time together as a couple.

8. **Living Simply.** Successful couples consciously simplify their lives. They limit activities that reduced family time, especially TV and outside activities, and also outside commitments. The study couples also talked about the importance of controlling finances so as not to have too many unnecessary expenditures.

They follow Stephen Marche's advice about keeping the house clean and presentable without being fanatics about it. They also use time-saving strategies to make life a little more efficient and a little less complicated.

9. **Making Decisions Proactively.** Being proactive in decision making is most important. Successful couples are vigilant in not allowing the pace of their lives to control them. They are proactive about keeping in control of their various responsibilities. They set and maintain a clear sense of priorities, which allows them to make good decisions about their marriage, children, family, and careers. They routinely engage in conscious and careful decision making in which they are both involved, making choices that are consistent with their priorities. These couples keep their eye on the bigger picture and stay aware of the consequences of their decision making.

10. **Valuing Time.** Successful couples try to remain aware of the value of time. They think about their time as a valuable commodity and resource to be spent with great care, and tend to be protective of it. The study couples reported finding themselves oriented to the present and highly focused on making the most of each day.

The couples in this study were predominantly well-educated, middle-class couples with at least one child under the age of twelve. The couples had to describe themselves as successful in balancing family and work, and both partners had to agree to participate. While it's possible that the results of this study cannot be generalized to include all couples, the core values here seem fairly universal. Perhaps the way these general strategies are carried out in your relationship will be different, but the intended goals of each strategy do seem pertinent to all.

HUSBANDS CAN AFFECT THEIR WORKPLACE CULTURE

It is important to remember that, as a husband, you can affect your workplace; you don't have to simply adapt your life to the demands of your job situation. One *Washington Post* article, "How Do You Erase the Taboo of Paternity Leave?" describes a group of about twenty Twitter employees who gathered at the office to swap stories about becoming new parents.[9] They shared stories, lamented their lack of sleep, talked about how to limit email intrusions, etc.—but what made this conversation unusual was that the participants were not working mothers, they were men attending a "Dads on Leave" roundtable. This is a big deal . . . making it okay for dads to talk about parenting, family leave, and their jobs. (See the sidebar on challenging the taboo of paternity leave for a look at what some of the more progressive companies today offer their male employees following the birth of a child.)

Challenge the Taboo of Paternity Leave

The following companies break the traditional mold by offering new fathers in their employ lengthy paid paternity leaves:

Twitter: ten weeks

Richard Branson's Virgin investment firm: one year

Johnson & Johnson: nine weeks

Patagonia: eight weeks

Google: twelve weeks

Bank of America: twelve weeks

Jena McGregor. "How do you erase the taboo of paternity leave?" *Washington Post.* June 18, 2015.

Some progressive companies are nudging fathers to take time off for parenting. But most companies are not. Only about 13 percent of US full-time employees had access to paid family leave in 2012. However, things are changing. Companies have begun to understand that they must compete for talented young male employees who want more flexibility and greater involvement in their children's lives. Pricewaterhouse Coopers renamed its program "parental leave" to avoid the gender norms associated with previously referring to primary and nonprimary caregivers and to nudge fathers to take advantage of the benefit.

That said, men are going to have to continue to fight for the right to parental leave in the workplace. Here are a few suggestions for how to do this successfully:[10]

- ✦ Find ways to be more open about the importance of balance in your life.

- ✦ Promote the idea of "parental leave" rather than maternity or paternity leave. (When men see other men taking leave to be with family, it has an impact.)

- ✦ Ask for a medical certificate if you need time off to care for a sick child.

- ✦ Show that you value workplace flexibility by suggesting it as a recruitment incentive.

- ✦ Make it an election issue. If men want greater workplace flexibility, they need to let political parties know it's important.

- ✦ Fight for it collectively. Share your strategies in fighting for a better deal at work; discuss it with mentors, write about it in a newsletter, share articles on social media, and get it on the agenda at every forum possible.

- ✦ Support other men. Don't laugh along the next time a man is called "pussy-whipped" for leaving early so he can see his daughter's school play. When a male colleague takes a day off to care for his sick child, support him. Hopefully he will support you back in the future.

- ✦ Keep fighting, despite the backlash.

Balancing family and work is where negotiating collaboratively with your partner around the things of great value in your individual lives and your life together pays off. Challenging gender stereotypes and becoming more self-reflective will greatly enhance your ability to take on the challenge of how you and your spouse create and maintain a balance between family and work that works for both of you.

CHAPTER 8 ——————————

T
A Figure out what kind of marriage you want: traditional, romantic, HIP?

K
E Learn to recognize when you're automatically doing gender (this will take some work!).

A
W Be intentional about achieving the kind of work-family balance you want; talk about it
A with your spouse on an ongoing basis.

Y
S Managing household tasks, work, childcare, and caring for each other requires that you and your spouse rethink traditional ideas.

Be prepared to negotiate and renegotiate regularly with your spouse about work-family balance.

There are successful strategies you can use to create and maintain balance in your marriage.

Husbands need to be proactive about everything from making changes in the workplace to attitudes regarding parental leave and work-family balance in general.

9

Sharing Parenting

Every human culture seems to believe that children bring happiness. When people think about parenting, they tend to conjure up idealized images of perfect children. Even when prospective parents understand that raising a child will be painstakingly difficult, they tend to think quite happily about parenthood, which is why most of us eventually leap into it.

For those of you invested in a commitment to raising children together, this chapter will look at both the bad news and the good news about parenting. I will introduce Marc and Amy Vachon, who have made the commitment to equally share parenting, household chores, and work—in other words, they are a couple dedicated to finishing the revolution. I also will talk about fatherhood in the twenty-first century (hint: it will be different). Finally, I have a note about choosing not to be a parent.

A CAUTIONARY TALE

Jennifer Senior, who is a contributing editor at *New York Magazine*, wrote about the impact children have on parents—a switch from the usual tale about the impact parents have on their children—in a great article called "All Joy and No Fun: Why Parents Hate Parenting" in 2010, which she followed up in 2014 with a book entitled *All Joy and No Fun: The Paradox of Modern Parenting*.[1] In both, Senior notes that from the perspective of the species, it's perfectly understandable why people have children. From the perspective of the individual, however, it may seem more of a mystery. Senior cites several researchers who note that parenting can be less than pleasurable:

✦ Daniel Kahneman, a Nobel Prize–winning behavioral economist, found that childcare ranked sixteenth in list of pleasurable activities (even housework was ranked higher).

✦ British economist Andrew Oswald found that among tens of thousands of Brits with children compared to those without, it wasn't that children made couples less happy—they just didn't make them *more* happy.

✦ Sociologist Robin Simon from Wake Forest University found that parents are more depressed than nonparents.

✦ Daniel Gilbert, Harvard professor of psychology and best-selling author of *Stumbling on Happiness*, notes that while we refer to children as "bundles of joy," they are not actually a source of happiness. "Once people have kids, there's a downturn in happiness," Gilbert says, and it isn't reversed until the kids move out. "Of course, we love our kids," said Gilbert. "I never said don't have kids." Still, the scientific data is tough to refute!

Kids: "You Can't Just Leave Them in Your Backyard."

This is a quote from a young woman in an article entitled "Millennials Plan to Trade Kids for Careers—But It Doesn't Have to Be That Way." Here is the rest of the story:

> *Erin Wehmann, 28, can tell when she and her husband have been at work too long. They'll come home to find Jake and Macey, their 7-year-old lab mixes, moping around the house.*
>
> *While she doesn't like leaving them for long stretches, she knows that during those occasional 10- to 12-hour work days, her dogs have plenty of food and water and access to the doggy door.*
>
> *"But that's not like a kid," she said. "You can't just leave them in your backyard."*
>
> *Wehmann and her 30-year-old husband, Ben, who until recently was traveling three weeks out of the month for work, used to talk about having children, but now she has second thoughts.*
>
> *"I have been concerned . . . that I wouldn't be able to find a balance with adding kids to the mix," said Wehmann, who lives in Madison, Wisc., and works for a software company. "It's a struggle now to find a good balance between non-work obligations, being able to have hobbies, and spending time with my husband. To think of adding a child to that is definitely something that I can't imagine being able to juggle."*
>
> Sara Israelsen-Hartley. "Millennials Plan to Trade Kids for Careers—But It Doesn't Have to Be That Way." *Deseret National News.* March 16, 2014.

Senior reviewed a 2003 metastudy (study of studies) that found the usual result: Couples start out marriage with high marital satisfaction. Satisfaction goes down as the couple has children and rises again when the children leave home.

This result shows up regularly in marital relationship research. In addition, research shows that mothers are less happy than fathers, single parents are less happy than married parents, babies and toddlers are the hardest to parent, and each successive child produces increasing unhappiness.

Surprisingly, Senior found that research on parenting also shows that happiness decreases even if parents are well enough off to buy more childcare. Couples that become parents later in life may experience a greater sense of loss of freedom and loss of autonomy as they have children than their younger parent counterparts do. It may also be that the longer they wait to have children, the greater their expectations become about what kids will bring to them.

THE GOOD NEWS

The good news Senior describes is that newer research expands our understanding of the impact children have on us. For example, Matthew White and Paul Dolan, two British academics, show us why having kids may be a good idea after all.[2] They figured out that measuring happiness and satisfaction can be improved upon if you measure thoughts and not just feelings.

What White and Dolan found is based on a study of 625 participants who completed an online questionnaire about the activities they engaged in the previous day. These included such activities as eating, reading, spending time with children, watching TV, working, and commuting. Their findings confirmed other research measuring pleasure from these kinds of activities—i.e., that we spend a lot of time doing things we don't find pleasurable, including "work" and "shopping." "Time with children" ranked about midway along the pleasure scale, far below "outdoor activities" and "watching TV."

However, when the researchers had the participants rate the **reward**, rather than pleasure, derived from engaging in these same activities, "work" was the top scorer, with "time with children" not far behind. White and Dolan concluded that if you look only at the pleasure of an activity, you will conclude that you have a bad time engaging in many of them. But, when you consider how *rewarding* some of those less "fun" activities—like spending time with your children—are, you will conclude that you are having a good time. **So, spending time with children may not always be pleasurable, but it can be quite rewarding.**

Daniel Gilbert also reminds us that children offer "moments of transcendence" that make up for the difficult hours we spend with them. I recall visiting a museum with my three children to see a display of architects' ideas of future cities in space years ago. I went around with the older two, Chris and Ari, oohing and aahing, commenting on how remarkable these designs were. My then three-year-old daughter, Gabrielle, soon went off on her own, saying "remarkable, remarkable," as she stood in front of each design. The other visitors looked in amazement at our young art appreciator. These are the moments, as parents, that remind us of the joys of having children.

CHOOSING TO HAVE CHILDREN

Historically, couples didn't typically stop to think about having children. It used to be that you just had them; doing so was a given. But things are different now. Having and raising children has become an intentional activity; thus, it has become one of the most important things you can discuss and negotiate with your partner.

Beyond the usual things to think about—e.g., how you will work together to be effective parents—there are several larger issues to consider when you're thinking of becoming parents, according to author Christine Overall. In her book *Why Have Children: The Ethical Debate*, she argues that couples must also consider religious values, family values, and political values.[3] She also makes the surprising statement that the choice to have children calls for more careful thinking than the choice *not* to have children.

One of the issues Overall raises that is in tune with my approach in this book is the gendered nature of the decision to have children. While both you and your spouse should be involved in this decision, the choice you ultimately make has different meanings, implications, and risks for women than it does for men.

It is likely that each of you has your own ideas about having and caring for children. Before you move forward with having children, discuss and plan how you will work together to be effective parents, maintain gender equity, and sustain your relationship. Here are a few questions to ask one another:

1. Do we want children?
2. How will having children impact our lives?
3. What are our parenting philosophies?
4. What is our plan for having and raising our children?

THE NEW VIEW OF CHILDREN

While historically children were viewed as economic assets to their parents, in modern times childhood has increasingly become a protected, privileged time. Once college degrees became essential to getting ahead, children became subjects to be stimulated, instructed, and groomed for success. Senior describes it like this: "Kids, in short, went from being our staffs to being our bosses."[4]

Middle- and upper-income families tend to see their children as projects to be perfected. These families spend much time talking to children, answering questions with questions, and treating each child's thought as a special contribution. All of this is tiring work. Because parents feel they are putting their child at risk if they do not give them every advantage, however, they are willing to put in this effort.

Parents of all incomes, including working mothers, are spending more time with their children now. Yet—despite the fact that today's married mothers have less leisure time and want more—they still think they don't spend enough time with their children.

WHEN MOM AND DAD SHARE IT ALL

—

The research discussed above makes no reference to how parenting was managed by both mother and father. Probably most of the parent responders carried out the traditional roles of mothers and father, with mothers being primarily responsible for the childcare and fathers acting as helpers. This is frequently the case, regardless of whether the mother works or not.

How about a different view? One in which Mom and Dad share it all? Let me introduce you to Marc and Amy Vachon, who are committed to the idea of equally shared parenting.[5] They are well described in a 2008 *New York Times* article written by Lisa Belkin.

As Belkin tells it, the Vachons had designed their lives to prioritize their home life. The primary elements that helped them keep their lives afloat were lightened workloads and what Amy called the "bravery" to stand up to gender stereotypes.

Amy and Marc both worked thirty-two hours a week. They didn't divide up childcare and household tasks or divvy up specific responsibilities; nor did they keep track of who had done what. They each took responsibility for all aspects of parenting their two children on separate days. After their first child was born, the couple negotiated part-time schedules. Amy worked four days a week, Monday through Thursday, and Marc worked three ten-hour days, Monday, Wednesday, and Friday.

The couple divided their childcare responsibilities (getting the children up, feeding them, getting them to daycare or school, etc.) based on who was working what hours on a given day. For example, if their daughter wanted to schedule a visit with a friend (a play date) on Thursday, Marc took charge of the arrangements, because that was his day with the children. If their son had a play date on a Friday, Amy took responsibility.

Amy and Marc continually stayed alert and monitored how things were being shared between them. To avoid skirmishes about parenting or household tasks, they decided together what standards they were going to live with. For example, did they want to work toward a set nap schedule? Yes. Should their daughter's outfits match perfectly? No. How neat must the house be? (Remember, there is a case to be made for filth.). What constituted "doing the laundry"? How often did they need to vacuum?

For the Vachons, consensus emerged over time. They gave up being experts on anything, since such expertise usually involved a gender stereotype. They each had the privilege of doing things the "wrong" way—i.e., not their partner's way. (One example: Marc liked to "party in the tub" with their daughter when she was a baby, while Amy thought this was not the best way to ease a baby toward sleep.) They also did not compare themselves to what other mothers and fathers do. Marc once made the mistake of saying he did more around the house than any other man he knew. That kind of slip (and he did quickly realize that what he was saying *was* a slip), comparing himself to other men, is an easy trap to fall into when what you are trying to accomplish is difficult.

Sometimes the tasks that fell to Amy and Marc did fall along traditional gender lines. Amy had to work to accept, for example, that she was likely to be blamed if Marc failed to write thank-you notes. The point, for them, was to not default to these gender-driven roles but rather to think things through and talk about it. They worked hard to eliminate nagging, passive-aggressive forgetting, feigned incompetence, and honey-do lists from their relationship vocabulary.

As Lisa Belkin notes, many Marcs and Amys throughout the country are suggesting something simple: **gender should not determine the division of labor at home.**

TWENTY-FIRST-CENTURY FATHERHOOD IS GOING TO BE DIFFERENT

———

The men of today's generation want the "package deal" of marriage, fatherhood, and employment but find that it is hard to attain, according to Nicholas Townsend's 2010 book *Package Deal: Marriage, Work, and Fatherhood in Men's Lives.* [6] Men feel pressure to devote themselves to work and an equal pull to devote themselves to their children, wanting to be closer to their children than their fathers were to them. There are also increasing demands on fathers to be active parents if they want to stay involved with the mothers of their children.

Supporting the involvement of fathers in the care of their children challenges stale ideas about men as fathers. Fortunately, new research supports the idea that men, like women, are biologically prepared to be good parents.

THE MAKING OF A MODERN FATHER: IT'S THE HORMONES (AGAIN)

The newest research on men as fathers focuses on the role of hormones such as prolactin, which facilitates lactation in women and instigates parental behavior in male birds and mammals; cortisol, which is a well-known stress hormone but also a good indicator of mother's attachment to her baby; and testosterone, which is abundant in male animals during mating but decreases during nurturing. (We already know from Chapter 5 that testosterone is also related to solo sexual desire but not sex with your partner.) Oxytocin, which is released during childbirth, is a hormone that helps cement the bond between mother and baby. Vasopressin is another important bonding hormone. Let's look at some of the findings related to these hormones and being a father.

For a recent study, Drs. Anne Storey and Katherine Wynne-Edwards, biologists at Memorial University and

Queens University in Canada, took blood samples from thirty-four couples at different times during pregnancy and shortly after birth with the intention of assessing their levels of prolactin, cortisol, and testosterone.[7] The results showed: 1) prolactin levels increased by approximately 20 percent in the men in the study in the three weeks before their partners gave birth; 2) expectant fathers' cortisol levels were twice as high in the three weeks before birth than they had been earlier in pregnancy; and 3) testosterone levels decreased by 33 percent in fathers in the first three weeks after their child's birth.

Marital status and paternal responsibility may have a significant effect on levels of testosterone in men. Anthropologist Peter Gray, along with fellow researchers Ben Campbell of the University of Wisconsin and Peter Ellison of Harvard University, examined the effect of marital status on testosterone in East Africans.[8] They compared testosterone levels among single men, men married to one wife, and men married to multiple wives, and found that monogamously married men had significantly lower testosterone levels than did single men of similar age.

A second study conducted by this group examined the effect of fatherhood on the hormones testosterone, prolactin, oxytocin, cortisol, and vasopressin.[9] Gray and his team analyzed hormone concentrations from forty-three Jamaican men between eighteen and forty years old who were single, biological fathers who had a visiting relationship with their children, and biological fathers living with their youngest child. Testosterone levels were significantly lower in visiting fathers than in single men. In single men (not visiting children), prolactin levels were significantly lower than they were in visiting fathers who participated in a twenty-minute session with their children.

When Siri van Anders, whom you met in Chapter 5, studied the relationship between testosterone (T) and parenting, she found that rather than being directly linked to behavioral masculinity, T is better thought of as related to **competition** and **nurturance**—i.e., high T is associated with competition, while low T is associated with nurturance. This finding helps us make sense of the decrease in T in the men described in the cited studies; low testosterone decreases competition, thus increasing a man's ability to be a nurturer to his children.

Studies have also found that infant cries **increase** T. What is this about? As van Anders notes, we have this social schema of parenting being all lovey-dovey. However, parenting also requires defending our kids, if we think they are threatened in some way. This seems to account for the spike in T when a father hears his baby crying.

Remember, Van Anders argues that the typical healthy range of T found in men is high enough (even for the men with low testosterone) to support sexual desire. The lower T that's associated with being a father will not diminish your interest in sex, or your ability to perform well in bed.

THE BRAINS OF FATHERS

———

Researchers at Princeton led by Yevgenia Kozorovitskiy found enhancements in the prefrontal cortex of father marmosets.[10] Specifically, the neurons in this region showed greater connectivity in the area responsible for planning and memory (competencies necessary for good parenting). Neurons in the area were found to have more receptors for vasopressin, a hormone shown to prompt animal fathers to bond with offspring. Kozorovitskiy suggests that such neural enhancement may be the neural basis of parenting.

YOU CAN BE THE KIND OF FATHER YOU WANT TO BE

This new body of research suggests that paternal involvement in raising one's children is supported by your biology. This work challenges the notion offered by evolutionary psychologists that fathers are natural-born deadbeats, big on courtship, always on the lookout for the next big fling, and short on childrearing. Don't believe it. Steve Almond, a widely published short story writer and essayist, wrote an article in 2008 called "Bimbo Proof the Nursery" following the birth of his daughter.[11] While he did buy into the evolutionary myth of the "Dude Self" in this piece, Almond also did a serious job of reflecting upon how his Dude Self behavior might negatively impact his newly born daughter. He acknowledged, for example, that he is harming his daughter by "checking out" female celebrities like Paris Hilton and Lindsay Lohan. He believes that doing things like trolling the internet for a free version of the Paris Hilton sex video (which he did) has negative consequences for daughter. He believes it sends her the message that "Daddy loves sluts; be a slut, and Daddy will love you." He also argues that even if he "ogled Paris in private, he would still be contributing to the 'Culture of Paris'"—i.e., helping to shape a world in which young women win adulation for making porn videos instead of curing cancer or brokering peace in the Middle East or being a mom.

In conflict with Almond's Dude Self is his Dad Self—the guy who has to worry about the survival of his wife and daughter. Almond says his Dad Self regards women differently. He has to think about the kind of world in which he'd like his daughter to grow up, and especially how he would like other males to treat her—which is to say, not as a sexual chew toy but with kindness and respect.

WHEN THERE IS STRONG SOCIAL SUPPORT

Jennifer Senior describes a well-designed study, done with European parents, that found that countries with stronger welfare systems produce more children—and happier children. Of course, such a finding should not be a surprise. Here are the benefits that such countries provide parents:

- A year of paid maternity leave
- Affordable childcare
- Free education
- Free healthcare

Judith Warner, author of *Perfect Madness: Motherhood in the Age of Anxiety*, notes that in the United States compared to European countries, we put our energy into being perfect parents instead of into effecting political change that would make family life better for everyone.[12] Marriage historian Stephanie Coontz, meanwhile, talks about the barriers parents are up against as they try to change the child-rearing rules.[13] Coontz says that couples need to be less indignant with each other and more indignant with society. Our work demands, our familial infrastructure, and the schedules of schools and offices remain fixed in a two-parent, single-income world. Jennifer Senior says more generous government policies, a sounder economy, and a less pressured culture that values good rather than perfect kids—these would certainly make parents happier.

SOME PRACTICAL ADVICE

Scads of websites and books focus on bringing up healthy and happy children. Don't forget, if you do have children, you will get lots of advice, good and bad, from friends and relatives—and you will want to try to seek out the best of the bunch. How do you discern between the good and the bad? Here are a few tips from on how to sort out parenting resources from Nancy Heath, PhD, director of human development and family studies programs at American Public University:[14]

The advice you receive should build your confidence as a parent, not make you feel inadequate.

There are few ironclad rules about how to be a good parent, so there is no reason for any resource to take a critical attitude toward how you are raising your children.

Seek at least one resource that talks about normal developmental milestones.

But don't get too hung up on what's "normal." Use these developmental milestones as general guides, not as fast rules by which to measure your child.

Assess whether the resource is based on scientifically established child development principles.

Authors have their own approach to raising children, which should be grounded in proven research. If the advice has no basis in solid research, *choose another book*.

Choose resources that help you enjoy your child.

Dr. Heath believes that the best parenting advice of all is to have fun with your kids. Remember, developing a trusting relationship with your children is more important than managing and controlling them.

A bit of personal advice about children: Children are not more important than the adults in a family. They are dependent on us for virtually everything, but that does not elevate their importance in the family. On the other hand, we must also remember that they have full status in the family; undervaluing them is just as bad as overvaluing them!

CHOOSING NOT TO HAVE A CHILD

According to recent surveys, women without children are not anomalies. The 2014 US Census Bureau's Current Population Survey shows that 47.6 percent of women between fifteen and forty-four have never had children. This figure is the highest percentage of childless women recorded since 1976, when the bureau started tracking this data.

Dr. Gail Goss, a parenting expert, notes in a 2014 article in the *Huffington Post* that some young women are not interested in motherhood.[15] Some may even not be suited for motherhood because of their history or temperament. Goss believes we should applaud women who know and acknowledge up front that they cannot or are not willing to dedicate a portion of their lives to childcare. Elizabeth Plank at MIC.com (a liberal media company focused on news for the millennial generation), however, says that when it comes to this topic, women can't win.[16] As she notes, "Despite the fact that having children remains a substantial burden in today's society, women—working or not—are treated as selfish or strange for choosing not to raise a family."

Moira Weigel wrote a provocative article in the May 10, 2016, edition of the *Guardian* entitled "The Foul Reign of the Biological Clock."[17] In it, she discusses the insidious concept of the biological clock and its negative impact on women. Women in many times and places have felt pressure to bear children. But the idea of the biological clock is a particularly malevolent, and recent, invention. The concept—

which is a metaphor, by the way, not an actual biological reality—was invented in the late 1970s by writer Richard Cohen.

Weigel notes that we are used to thinking about metaphors like the biological clock as if they were not metaphors at all but simply neutral descriptions of facts about the human body. The metaphor of the biological clock, however, has as much to do with culture as with nature. And its cultural role has been to counteract the effects of women's liberation.

I'll leave you here with the words of Elizabeth Plank: "Young women may be the ones delaying having children, but politicians are the ones who need to get their act together. While they delay taking an initiative to change our flawed family leave policies, millennials' aversion to children will likely continue to grow. Rather than shun women who make an arguably logical decision not to have kids, we should reserve our judgment for policymakers who fail to bring us into the twenty-first century when it comes to family planning."

CHAPTER 9 ——————

**T
A
K
E
A
W
A
Y
S**

Parenting is both difficult and rewarding.

Equally shared parenting is a real challenge.

More and more couples are striving to share care and work equally because it is better for everyone.

Newer research shows that men, like women, are biologically prepared to be good fathers.

There is nothing wrong with choosing not to have children, and there is no such thing as a biological clock.

American society is woefully lacking in its support for children and families.

There are many good books on parenting; the ones worth reading are based on scientific research and help build your confidence as a parent—they don't make you feel inadequate.

PART V

—

HOW THE REVOLUTION CAN STALL

10

Gender Traps

Despite your commitment to gender equality, there are many ways your revolution can get stalled. Throughout this book, I have challenged old ideas about gender and explained how such ideas will stop you from achieving an equitable relationship. I have also challenged you to be more self-reflective and have given you some tools to do this. The more you use these ideas as you attempt to cocreate an equitable relationship with your spouse, the more resilient you will be when you come against the many traps out there, particularly those that are driven by gender stereotypes.

Here, I will discuss several traps that I think are common: the pull toward a traditional marriage arrangement; how men and women talk; feeling like your masculinity is being challenged; being too nice; and being resistant to change.

THE PULL TOWARD A TRADITIONAL MARRIAGE

The practical impact of childbearing and childrearing continues to have greater consequences for women than for men, even for those couples who hold egalitarian ideologies. Women still retain primary responsibility for children, even when they have full-time jobs. Trying to combine work and family leads many women to prefer giving up their career aspirations because of the difficulty of managing both. For the most part, husbands nowadays are typically supportive of their wives' decisions, but they are still less likely to offer to sacrifice their own work commitments. While younger fathers are more willing to take on childcare responsibilities, they are less likely to take on traditional household chores. For women who decide to opt out of the workforce while their children are young, returning to work after the children are in school seems like a good option; however, by this time the husband's earning power has often so outstripped theirs that wives come to think of their salary as extra money rather than as a major contribution to the family. And as Gerson found in her study, women will choose economic independence over marriage if they cannot create an equitable arrangement with their partner.

The *Harvard Business Review* study of graduates that I described in Chapter 8 pointed out how difficult it is for millennials to maintain their expectation about their careers and home life.[1] While the study found that both women and men graduates of the Harvard Business School had about equal expectations about how their careers and home life would go, the actual lives of the women who participated in the study did not live up to those expectations. As previously noted, these are bright, well-educated women and men who, despite their good intentions, fell back into traditional roles once they married and had children.

One of the reasons I push for shared parenting is that lack of good support for childcare is one of the major reasons couples fall back on traditional approaches once children arrive. Lack of flexibility in their work setting is another major reason for such a pull toward traditional marriage. In the Harvard study I just referenced, one female graduate—a mother of two and the founder and chief executive of a company—did report that her career and home life matched her expectations. She said she was up front about her career goals with her husband, they "are on the same page," and they "actively manage" balancing jobs and childcare. When you marry, being clear on the obstacles you will face in the years to come is crucial, as is putting in the work so you're prepared to deal with them.

OLD IDEAS ABOUT MEN AND WOMEN

To get beyond gender stereotypes in communication, we need to say what they are. Let's start with a few of the popular stereotypes about how men and women communicate:

+ Communication matters more to women than it does to men.

+ Women talk more than men.

+ Women have better verbal skills than men.

+ Men talk to get things done; women talk to make emotional connection.

✦ Men talk about things; women talk about people, relationships, and feelings.

✦ Men use language to provide information, preserve their independence and compete to maintain status; women use language to enhance cooperation, reflecting their preference for harmony.

✦ Women tend to soften their statements by using tag phrases (e.g., "don't you think," "if you don't mind"); men are more direct.

Since the publication of John Gray's *Men Are from Mars, Women Are from Venus* and Deborah Tannen's *You Just Don't Understand*, these old ideas about how men and women communicate have become dogma—unquestioned articles of faith. Tannen is a well-respected linguist who has publicly defended her assertions about these communication differences between men and women. These generalizations, however, are widely disputed by thirty-some years of research on language, communication, and the sexes.

Alice Freed, Professor Emerita of Linguistics at Montclair State University, performed a close study of Tannen's work—and found that Tannen is an apologist for men. She excuses their insensitivities in her examples as part of their "need for independence."[2] She emphasizes the importance of women adjusting to men's need for status and independence. In *You Just Don't Understand*, for example, she shares a story about Josh, who invites an old high school friend who is visiting from another town to spend a weekend with him and his wife, Linda. The visit is to begin immediately upon Linda's return from a weeklong business trip. Josh does not discuss the invitation with her before he extended it to his friend. Linda is upset by his failure to do so; her feelings are hurt.

According to Tannen, Linda's hurt feelings would disappear if only she understood that for Josh to ask permission would imply that he is not independent, not free to act on his own. He would feel controlled by Linda's wish to be consulted. This is a glaring example of a person of authority buying into the old gender stereotype that women must defer to men in order not to threaten their egos.

Cross-checking with your partner is not "seeking permission." It is being willing to negotiate with your spouse about what works for both of you. If Josh feels controlled, he needs to take an inventory of that experience. (See Chapter 3, "Taking Care of Your Personal Issues," for how to take a personal inventory of your reactions.)

By the way, Tannen also relies on the old notion that hurt feelings are what is important to Linda. What is actually important to Linda, however, is that Josh is unwilling to negotiate with her about what he wants.

Tannen is using her status as an academic to promote stereotypic ideas based on anecdotal material like the story described above. She uses these anecdotal stories as a basis for making sweeping generalizations about men and women.

In *The Female Brain*, published in 2006, Louann Brizendine, MD, claims that women say about twenty thousand words a day, while men say about seven thousand.[3] This was such a wonderful sound bite that mirrored the stereotype that women talk three times as much as men that it was reported in newspapers around the world.

Mark Liberman, a linguistic professor at the University of Pennsylvania, decided to investigate the research that supported such a claim because he was skeptical about Brizendine's source.[4] What he found was that the above statement about how much men and women talk came from a self-help book, with no academic citation referencing the statement. Reviewing other similar findings that women talk much more than men yielded word counts for women ranging from four thousand to twenty-five thousand words—again, with no research supporting such statements.

Dr. Brizendine retracted her statement when Dr. Liberman pointed out his research in a newspaper article, noting the statement would be deleted from future editions. However, the damage was done; this much-publicized stereotypic sound bite that women talk three times more than men will linger in people's memories and get recycled in conversations for years, maybe even decades, to come. The retraction will not make the same impression. **This is how myths about men and women acquire the status of facts.**

In a review of fifty-six studies cited in Deborah Tannen's work, linguistics researcher Deborah James and social psychologist Janice Drakich found that only two of the studies on male and female conversational styles showed that women talked more than men, while thirty-four of them found men talked more than women.[5] Sixteen of the studies found they talked the same amount, and four showed no clear pattern. What James and Drakich did find in reviewing these studies was the amount people talk is related to the status of the person and the kind of situation in which a conversation occurs. They found that in more formal or public settings, the person who talks more is the person of higher status. In these kinds of situations, that person is usually a man. Women, in contrast, are seen as having higher status in the domestic realm, accounting for why some studies show women as talking more. Unfortunately, "status" turns out to be a code for "gender" in this case.

Unfortunately, most of us do not read scientific journals; we read popular books like Gray's and Tannen's. Because of this, even when a retraction is made about a gender stereotype published in the popular press (e.g., the statement that women say twenty thousand words a day while men say about seven thousand), the false belief continues because by the time the retraction is issued, it has already become part of the stereotyped narrative about women and men—usually to the detriment of women.

MEN ARE FROM ~~MARS~~ EARTH, WOMEN ARE FROM ~~VENUS~~ EARTH

———

A 2007 study conducted by Bobbi Carothers, a senior data analyst at Washington University, and Harry Reis, a professor of psychology at the University of Rochester, demonstrates the need for the Mars/Venus theories about the sexes to come back to earth.[6]

Reis notes that people think about the sexes as **distinct categories**. Remember, the first question parents are asked about their newborn is, "Boy or girl?" Together, Carothers (the lead author of the study) and Reis pointed out that it is not at all unusual for men to be empathic and women to be good at math. As Carothers says, "Sex is not nearly as confining a category as stereotypes and even some academic studies would have us believe."

Carothers and Reis reanalyzed data from thirteen studies that had shown significant sex differences, and they collected their own data on a variety of psychological indicators, such as relationship interdependence, intimacy, sexuality, agreeableness, emotional stability, and conscientiousness, as well. Then, using three separate statistical procedures, they looked for measures that could reliably distinguish a person as male or female. Here is what they found:

+ On characteristics such as height, shoulder breadth, arm circumference, and waist-to-hip ratio, men and women fall into distinct groups (called taxons).

+ Gender reliably predicts interest in stereotypic activities such as scrapbooking and cosmetics (women) and boxing and watching pornography (men).

These researchers looked at the data to see if they could separate the men from the women based on a particular psychological trait. This is what they found:

+ For most of the psychological traits, including fear of success, criteria for mate selection, and empathy, men and women are from the same planet.

- A given person—a man, for example—may score in a stereotypic way on one measure (say, aggression) and rank low on another stereotypic characteristic (like math ability).

- For psychological traits, the overlap between men and women is so great that the authors conclude that we cannot sort men and women into separate categories based on these traits.

Emphasizing inherent differences between the sexes—a practice that is certainly routine in the popular press and even in some academic circles—can be harmful in the context of a marriage relationship. Adhering to gender stereotypes gets in the way of looking at one's partner as an individual. When something goes wrong, it is too easy to blame the other partner because of his/her gender.

GENDER EQUALITY AND THREATENED MASCULINITY

Should you check with your wife to have a night out? Shouldn't you be able to make decisions for yourself? Should your wife question the choices you've made without checking with her first? Are you not the head of the household?

Your feelings of masculinity may play out consciously and subconsciously in your relationship with your wife. Becoming aware of this will help you prevent a stalled revolution in your marriage.

Here is how one newly married man described how these feelings can play out:

> *Shortly after tying the knot, a friend asked if I wanted to watch a football game at a local bar and grill. I hesitated. "Maybe. Let me check with the wife first." Then I quickly added, "I'm probably forgetting some plans we've already made, but if not, then I'm definitely in." The sinking feeling in my stomach begged two gnawing questions: First, did I give up my decision-making power at the wedding altar? And, second, did I lose some manhood along with it?*[7]

Being married gives you the chance to challenge your own, often quite subconscious, sense of masculinity or manhood. The traditional societal view of masculinity revolves around a set of core features that a man must demonstrate or aspire to demonstrate: power, authority, rationality, risk-taking, dominance, control, and suppression of emotions.

In marrying, you will be going from **independent** bachelor to **interdependent** married man. In being interdependent, you will share power and authority with your wife. This is not achieved by simply ceding authority to her; it is done be being willing to negotiate with your wife on the issues that arise in your marriage. When to check with each other before making a decision is one example. Sharing power and authority does not equate to a loss of masculinity; it has to do with the way in which you interact with one another.

IT'S THE FEMININE THING TO DO

———

As a wife, you can fall into the marital trap of being "nice" to your husband. Being nice can be a way of acting out society's instruction that women should be nurturing and caring toward others. Other qualities assumed to be female include: receptivity, being empathic, sharing, tenderness, and patience. Being nice gets translated into making unilateral accommodations to your husband. This "nice girl" approach is implicitly saying, "I will make sure you get what you want, even without your having to ask me for it."

This kind of niceness is a way of playing out more traditional views of how wives should act. It is also often based on your own insecurities, such as:

+ Not asserting what you want to avoid being criticized
+ Avoiding being assertive because you think that if you are nice to him, he will be nice to you
+ Not wanting to be thought of as "too aggressive"
+ Not wanting your husband to think you're not being a "good girl"

Being nice can also be a self-protective strategy that can have a negative effect on your relationship.[8] Being nice tends to generate a feeling of **entitlement** that gets hidden behind the notion of **fairness** in your marriage. Here are some examples of entitlements that can come from you feeling that you are owed something from your spouse because you are being nice:

✦ ***Because I have sacrificed.*** "I gave up my career to raise our kids, so you have to consent to [*fill in the blank*]."

✦ ***Because I do more.*** Both husband and wife are susceptible to this kind of entitlement. A husband might say, "Since I work longer hours than you do, you should go to the market." A wife might reply, "Since I work and do the cooking, you should go." Each has his/her own score-keeping system.

✦ ***Because I don't ask for much.*** This entitlement comes from seeing oneself as the more generous and accommodating partner. "I go along with your way most of the time, so when I ask for something, you should grant it."

✦ ***Because I did something nice.*** "I said 'I love you' twice this week. You have to do the same for me."

Accommodating your husband's desires without first negotiating your own is disrespectful to you and misleading to him. He does not know that you are being nice. He may come to think, *This is great! My wife loves everything I do!*—and over time, he may come to expect that you will accommodate everything he wants and cease taking into consideration what is important to you. You, in turn, are likely to become increasingly unhappy, thinking he is selfish, overbearing, and self-centered.

In order for your marriage to work, you must invest yourself in it. And this is not about being nice. It is about being *something*. Being something means you have wishes and wants, things you desire—things that are not determined solely by your gender.

WHEN HUSBANDS RESIST CHANGE

Because the gender revolution is an unfinished revolution, wives are more likely to want an egalitarian relationship than husbands. When wives raise issues, therefore, it is likely that they want some kind of change, and husbands, quite without conscious awareness, can become resistant to that change.

Pay attention to how you react when your wife raises an issue for discussion. Is your first tendency to resist? (Note: You cannot put your wife in the position of identifying and naming your resistance. You will perceive her as criticizing you, and you will become more resistant, upping your resistance tactics. This is something you need to acknowledge on your own.)

John Gottman is a well-known psychologist who has researched, written about, and counseled husbands and wives.[9] He found that there is an 81 percent chance that a marriage will self-destruct if a husband is not willing to share authority and power with his wife. Other marital researchers have studied how this resistance plays out in the marital relationship, and they've found that a pattern develops when husbands are resistant to letting their wives influence them. This is called a "demand-withdraw" dynamic; however, "demand" is not where it starts. The demand-withdraw pattern usually starts when a wife seeks some sort of change in the relationship (as noted above, it is most often the wife who seeks change in the marital relationship, because husbands are more likely to be satisfied with traditionally defined relationships). When she seeks change, she finds that her husband engages in some avoidance tactic—i.e., he resists responding to the request. Over repeated instances of this interaction, her requests become more insistent—they become demands in his mind—and this, to him, justifies his increased resistance. This is what sets up the ongoing demand-withdraw pattern.[10]

Gottman has found in his research that more than 80 percent of the time, it is the wife, not the husband, who will bring up a marital issue. If you find yourself trying to avoid discussing issues your wife raises, you are likely using one of four general tactics identified by Gottman: **stonewalling**, **defensiveness**, **criticism**, or **contempt**. These are the typical tactics resistant husbands use when their wives approach them with a request, complaint, problem, or issue. Here is a brief description of these tactics with examples:[11]

Stonewalling.

Gottman says that the stonewaller is the husband in 85 percent of marriages. You are stonewalling when you withdraw from an interaction with your wife by getting quiet or shutting down. You may turn away, stop making eye contact, cross your arms, or leave the room. Here are two examples:

+ Your wife asks you to join a family outing on a sports-heavy weekend. You respond with folded arms, muttering, "Whatever."

+ You accuse your wife of nagging when she tries to raise a concern.

Defensiveness.

When you act defensively, you are essentially saying to your wife that she is the problem, and you are not. Here are two examples:

+ Your wife wants to talk about keeping on budget, raising issues such as how much money you spend on electronic devices. You respond, "How about how much money you spend on clothes!"

+ You are reading when your wife calls from the other room, "What are you doing?" Your response is, "What's wrong with me just reading for a while?"

Criticism.

A criticism and a complaint are not the same thing. A complaint addresses a specific action; it is describing something that is occurring. A criticism is a characterization of your wife; it is about her, not about the situation. Here are two examples of the difference between a complaint and a criticism:

+ A *criticism* is, "I hate it when you don't let me know that you are going to be late. You are really self-centered." A *complaint/request* is, "I get worried when

I don't know where you are, would you call me when you are going to be late?"

+ A *criticism* is, "We never go out to have a good time; you are such a homebody; you're no fun!" A *complaint/request* is, "I really like to go out more than you seem to. Can we talk about this, maybe go out this weekend?"

Contempt.

Contempt is a big one. Contempt implies that your wife is not deserving of your respect when it comes to her wishes and wants. It is expressed in insults, name-calling, hostile humor, mockery, tone of voice, and facial expression. Contempt will eat away at your relationship—rapidly and painfully. Here is an example of contempt:

+ In a discussion over who is doing what around the house, you roll your eyes at your wife. You think about all the things you do for her and the lack of acknowledgement you get. You finally say in a sarcastic voice, "I'm sure you do so much more than I do. I am so happy to just be your handyman around the house!"

Husbands historically have used the above tactics to resist being influenced by their wives, avoid looking at themselves, and/or protect their masculinity when they perceive it as being challenged.

As a young husband, you have the personal power to do things differently; you don't have to define your masculinity in terms of resistance to your wife's influence. You can become more aware of your own reactions to your wife, learn to be more self-reflective, strive to collaborate, and, most important, learn to negotiate win-win solutions. Practicing these new approaches can be your part in creating an equitable, sustainable, and satisfying marriage.

MALE PRIVILEGE

——

Privilege is about advantages you have that *you think are normal.*[12] This is why when your wife (or anyone else) accuses you of being privileged, you are likely to get defensive— or, if you do have some idea of what male privilege is but don't know what to do about it, to feel guilty.

Neither defensiveness nor guilt is helpful to your marriage. So let's see what can be done about *male privilege.*

First, let's define privilege and then see how this notion applies to men, in general. Privilege can be defined as a set of **unearned benefits** given to people who fit into a specific group. It is society, at large, that grants privilege to people because of certain aspects of their identity, such as race, class, gender, sexual orientation, language, etc. More specifically, male privilege is a set of privileges that are given to men as a class in relation to women as a class. While each individual man will experience privilege differently due to his specific position in the social hierarchy, every man benefits from male privilege.

For men to have some privileged status vis-à-vis women is considered to be the norm by most societies in the world. Take, for example, a married woman who keeps her family name upon getting married. Equality in this instance is a husband keeping his name and the wife keeping hers. Because the norm privileges men, however, this woman will have to explain why she chose not to take her husband's name. Popular culture can label her behavior as emasculating her husband. How a woman might feel about giving up something that has been part of her identity since birth is not considered.

Examples of Male Privilege

Here are a few items considered examples of male privilege that are so much a part of what we consider normal and usual that we must make a list of them:

- If I choose not to have children, my masculinity will not be called into question.
- If I have children and a career, no one will think I'm selfish.
- I am far less likely to face sexual harassment at work.
- My grooming regimen is relatively cheap and consumes little time.
- If I buy a new car, chances are I'll be offered a better price than a woman would be offered.
- If I am not conventionally attractive, the disadvantages are relatively small and easier to ignore.
- I can be loud with little fear of being called a shrew. I can be aggressive with no fear of being called a bitch.

- I can be confident that the ordinary language of day-to-day existence will always include my sex ("All men are created equal").
- My ability to make important decisions will never be questioned depending on what time of the month it is.
- Every major religion in the world is led primarily by people of my own sex. Even God is pictured as male.

Adapted from Barry Deutsch's "The Male Privilege Checklist." https://www.cpt.org/files/US%20-%20Male%20Privilege%20Checklist.pdf.

One man struggling to understand the concept of male privilege once said, "Men don't often experience gender-based street harassment, but that's not a privilege. It's something everyone should expect."

Correct. Everyone *should* expect and has a right to be treated that way. **The problem is, certain people *aren't* treated that way.**

Your job in your marriage is to be willing to be more self-aware about how you are affected by societal male privilege. You, individually, are not to blame. Privilege is not your fault; it's not something you chose. But if you want an egalitarian and satisfying relationship with your wife, you must understand that you benefit from male privilege, be willing to work with your wife on noticing when male privilege gets in the way, and push back against your privilege.

KEEPING THE REVOLUTION GOING

There are things you can do to avoid falling into the patterns that will limit your efforts to create a new way of being married. Here are a few of them:

Pay attention to times of transition in your life.

Transitions are changes in status that commonly include leaving school, starting a first job, forming an independent household, getting married, and becoming a parent. If you wish to create a life plan that includes a commitment to an egalitarian marriage, pay attention to how you and your spouse make decisions at these times. These decisions can easily be influenced by old ideas about how things should work for husbands and wives.[13]

For wives, this list includes:

+ Viewing your work as a job rather than a career

+ Having insufficiently established stable employment, particularly in your chosen career path

+ Delaying your education in the context of a committed relationship, perhaps due to family planning, while your husband goes to school

+ Viewing your own income as "extra" money because your husband has greater income potential

+ Opting for "pink collar" jobs known to have glass
  ceilings

+ Seeing marriage and having children as an
  acceptable alternative to a less-than-satisfactory
  career trajectory

Here is the list for husbands:

+ Worrying that you'll be seen as not fully
  committed to your job if you take time off for
  family

+ Facing limitations in your career if you are not
  seen as fully committed to your job

+ Not hearing other men talk about their families
  at work

+ Believing that what you do is who you are

+ Believing that women are better at taking care of
  children

Don't fall into the trap of viewing your wife's decision to be a stay-at-home mother as her individual choice.

It is too easy for both husbands and wives to see decisions
about work and family arrangements as due to individual
preferences, even convincing yourselves that these decisions
have been made by the two of you. Remember, being supportive of your wife's decision about family and work is not
the same thing as truly negotiating such arrangements. This
subconsciously places the responsibility for work–family outcomes on her.

Be up front.

Remember the Harvard study I cited earlier in which Harvard Business School (HBS) graduates reported whether their career and home life matched their expectations?[13] If you'll recall, one of the female participants—a mother of two and the founder and chief executive of a company—said that her expectations had indeed been met. Her explanation of how this was achieved: From the very beginning of her relationship with her husband, she was up front about her career goals. As a result, she and her husband "are on the same page" and they "actively manage" the balancing of jobs and childcare. It is a good idea to be up front from the beginning of your relationship about work and family issues. In fact, this is something you should do throughout your marriage, because there is always a strong pull toward a traditionally defined relationship. The follow-up to being up front is actively managing your life together.

Push to Negotiate Everything.

Because marriage has been organized around gender, individual wants and desires are viewed in terms of marital roles. That is, what you want is viewed in terms of being a wife (and mother) and being a husband (and father). As a wife, you want to take care of the children because that is an inherently female thing to do. As a husband, you like to work because that is an inherently male thing to do. These things are not negotiated; they are assigned per the traditional view of wife and husband roles. In order for you to have a satisfying, sustainable, and equal marriage, you must push to negotiate the individual wants and desires that flow from your individual and joint life plans, not from gender scripts. Don't get me wrong: gender attributes may shape wants and desires. But the fact that something you want might be gender related (a "man thing" or a "woman thing") does not take precedence over negotiating such wishes and wants in the context of your marriage. Individual wants are negotiated based on principles of collaborative negotiation, independently of whether such wants are related to gender. Neither of you can use gender as an excuse not to negotiate.

CHAPTER 10 ————————

TAKEAWAYS

A traditional marriage is the "default" mode, particularly at times of transition in your lives.

Both of you must buy into the idea that masculinity and femininity are not tied to what you do in your marriage.

Husbands must be aware when they feel their sense of masculinity is being threatened.

Wives must work hard to remain committed to their careers.

Husbands must notice when they use the strategies of stonewalling, defensiveness, criticism, and contempt to resist change.

Wives must remember to not be too nice.

Husbands must work to acknowledge how they benefit from male privilege.

By being acutely aware of these gender traps, you can keep the revolution going.

11

When Your Spouse Is
Mentally Ill

I have talked about how to consciously consider and analyze the personal issues you bring to your marriage. Everyone has such personal issues; we collectively describe them as our insecurities. Using the methods described in this book, you can learn to manage such insecurities and lessen their impact on your marriage. However, this approach to an equitable and sustainable marriage is not the way to deal with significant emotional and/or mental impairments that a partner may have, such as bipolar disorder, debilitating anxiety, clinical depression, obsessive-compulsive disorder, schizophrenia, alcoholism, drug addiction, and serious personality disorders such as narcissism, paranoia, and borderline personality.

If your spouse is engaging in actions and behaviors that are detrimental to establishing a successful marriage beyond the general insecurities we all have and are responsible for managing, it's important to recognize that—and to respond to it appropriately. You may choose to stay in the marriage. You may find it necessary to think about how and when to divorce your mentally ill spouse. Either way, it's important to have some idea of what to do if you believe your partner is suffering from a mental/emotional illness.

HOW DO YOU KNOW?

———

In a *Huffington Post* article she wrote in 2012, Sandy Malone is right on target when she asks:[1]

> How do you know and what do you do when your wife or husband starts suffering from a psychological condition? How can you tell the difference between a series of bad days and a real problem? How is a husband or wife to know when their occasionally moody spouse has gone from having a 'glass-is-half-full attitude' to actually suffering from clinical depression?

When issues such as repetitious arguments, unfounded accusations, lengthy withdrawals from the relationship, unwillingness or inability to discuss important issues, and/or standoffs between the two of you persist despite your efforts to engage your spouse, you must consider the possibility that more serious problems are occurring than surface-level disagreements. Excesses in behaviors can also be warning signs —being obsessed with ritual cleanliness, withdrawing completely from sexual contact, staying up all night and not being able to get to work or care for the children the next day, and excessive drinking or drugging, to name a few. When problems like this continue to occur in your marriage despite your using all the tools provided in this book (i.e., looking at yourself first, making repeated attempts to identify issues that bother your spouse, and repeated attempts to negotiate), it may be that something other than marital disagreement is occurring.

If your spouse is depressed, anxious, or acting in ways they cannot control or don't understand, they may not be able to tell you about these distressing feelings, or may be fearful to do so. He/she may say, "I'm just stressed"—because "stressed" has become a catchall term to cover all kinds of difficulties.

It's natural to feel reluctant to directly address your concerns about your spouse's emotional and psychological well-being, especially if it's your desire to be supportive rather than confrontational. Furthermore, you probably don't know *how* to raise the concerns you have.

This chapter is a general guide to addressing concerns of mental illness in your spouse. First, I'll share some ideas about what to do about your concerns about your spouse's well-being. Second, I'll walk you through what you can do if you find your spouse is mentally ill and you do not want to leave the marriage (or have not yet made a decision about what you want to do). Finally, I'll explore the idea of divorcing a mentally ill spouse, if that's the path you choose.

TAKING THE FIRST STEP

So, what can you do if you think your husband or wife may be suffering from mental illness or serious psychological problems? You can take a page from what we have learned about confronting the problem of alcoholism or alcohol/drug addiction. Here are several suggested steps:

Do not confront your spouse during an argument.

Choose a good time to initiate a conversation with your spouse about his/her behaviors/actions that you are concerned about and/or are having a negative impact on you and your marriage.

Express your concerns.

Talk about your worries, trying not to lecture. Give the clearest examples you can about the problems you are experiencing, e.g., "When you get angry, you are not able/willing to tell me what you are angry about"; "We no longer have sex; I miss our intimacy"; "When you drink, you get sullen and won't talk to me." These kinds of clear statements directly state the problem and its negative results.

Find out what your spouse thinks in a neutral manner.

Ask him/her if these actions are a problem for him/her too. Wait for him/her to answer. If he/she agrees that he/she is having a problem, you may want to ask questions like, "Why do you think you are having a problem with _____?"; "What do you think you can do about _____?" If your spouse can acknowledge that he/she is having difficulties, you can begin to negotiate the next steps (e.g., seeking help).

If he/she refuses to address the problem, continue to work at it.

If your spouse denies that they have a problem, continue to express your concerns and address his/her excuses from a place of compassion rather than judgment.

Put limits on your relationship if you need to.

If your spouse is continually unwilling to get help and continues to exhibit problematic behaviors despite your efforts, you may need to set clear boundaries on your relationship. For example, tell him/her that you cannot spend time with her/him when they act in the problematic way you have described. It may come to telling him/her you need a break until they're willing to seek help.

Consider getting professional help.

If your spouse won't cooperate, make an appointment with a physician, psychiatrist, or psychologist that the two of you can go to together so that you can discuss the concerns you have about your spouse. If your spouse will not cooperate, go on your own to get further help and guidance on how to proceed.

You can be helpful and supportive to a mentally ill spouse, as long as he/she recognizes the illness and seeks ongoing treatment. You'll also find you can be more sympathetic to your spouse if you understand what is happening to him/her, and if he/she is willing to take major responsibility for managing the illness. Don't forget about getting help for yourself as well; maintaining your own emotional well-being is crucial!

ADVICE ON HOW TO LIVE WITH A MENTALLY ILL SPOUSE

———

Living with a spouse who is mentally ill will be challenging. The condition from which your spouse is suffering with will determine what steps you'll need to take in order to live with and to help him/her. I have provided a list of articles in Appendix D (at the end of this book) on dealing with spouses with specific illnesses (alcoholism, Asperger's, bipolar disorder, borderline personality disorder, depression, narcissism, paranoia, psychosis, and post-traumatic stress disorder [PTSD]). It is important to learn as much as you can about the diagnosed condition to know how to help you spouse manage his/ her illness and how to take care of yourself in the process.

In my practice, I found working with the spouses of mentally ill partners to be rewarding. I often found that I had more impact on the ill person by working with his/her spouse. I also found that the mentally ill party was often more responsive to his/her spouse than to direct interventions I made. This was particularly true of one couple I worked with. The husband was paranoid, and I worked with his wife to help her set limits on what she was willing to talk about—i.e., she would not listen to the paranoid ideas he wanted to talk about. In joint therapy sessions, I confirmed for them both that this was the appropriate thing to do. In individual sessions with the wife, I encouraged her to attend to the fears associated with her husband's paranoid ideas rather than using logic to combat the ideas themselves. Working in this manner with them allowed her to show caring instead of challenging him about his ideas. She was allowed to give up trying to talk her husband out of his mistaken ideas.

I found this approach of enlisting the well spouse as the helper in the marriage successful in other situations with a mentally ill spouse as well. In fact, this work turned out to be some of the most rewarding therapeutic work I have done in my career.

There are various ways to work on the marital relationship when your spouse is mentally or emotionally ill. In my experience, this work benefits both partners as individuals and supports the overall well-being of the relationship.

In the work I described above, the paranoid spouse never admitted to being paranoid. However, he was committed to the marriage and loved his spouse, who was virtually his only companion. If your spouse neither recognizes his/her illness nor is willing to seek individual or marital therapy, the situation for you is difficult. You must seek professional help for yourself in this situation, work hard to maintain your own work and social life, stay informed about your spouse's illness, and be sure to seek out personal support from friends and family. If your spouse continues to refuse to own their illness, however, it is likely that at some point, you will consider divorce.

WHEN TO CONSIDER DIVORCE

Deciding to divorce a spouse who has a mental illness is a painful and complex decision. There will be enormous social pressure and guilt in deciding to end your marriage to someone who is mentally ill. You took those wedding vows to be married "in sickness and in health," after all.

Here are some suggestions for you to consider if you ever find yourself in this situation.[2]

- Give yourself the time you need to make the decision to end your marriage; talk with trusted others and professionals.
- A legal separation may address concerns you have with breaking your marriage vows.
- Think in terms of a loving detachment that involves:
  - Recognizing the process will take time
  - Considering how to help your spouse to be self-sufficient
  - Creating a parenting plan for your children that keeps your spouse involved in a way that is safe and feasible
  - Not holding your spouse's condition against him/her to penalize him/her
  - Leaving without anger or resentment

The reason I've broached this subject in this chapter is to let you know that the methods described in this book are designed for those who deal with the usual emotional insecurities we all experience—insecurities that can be managed through self-reflection. These approaches to an equitable and sustainable marriage are not sufficient when it comes to dealing with significant emotional and/or mental impairments that a partner may have.

CHAPTER 11 ———————

T
A
K
E
A
W
A
Y
S

It is not easy to figure out if your spouse is mentally ill or psychologically impaired.

When nothing is working in your marriage, it may be time to start thinking that some form of mental illness is occurring.

You must take the first steps of talking with your spouse about the issues you're concerned about so you can find out what you are dealing with.

There are guides to living with a mentally ill spouse that can help you negotiate this difficult situation.

If the situation becomes intolerable, you may need to considering leaving.

Seek professional help when making a decision about whether to leave your marriage.

The methods described in this book deal with our usual insecurities about ourselves; they are not appropriate ways to deal with mental and emotional illness.

CONCLUSION

As a psychologist, I have taken on the task of looking at achieving an equitable marriage through the prism of psychological self-awareness. Becoming more insightful about yourself allows you to examine your marital relationship through the lens of collaborative negotiation. In learning to recognize and manage your own personal issues, you prepare yourself to be willing and able to engage collaboratively with your spouse. In doing so, you make it possible for both of you to accomplish your individual goals and to enhance the quality of your marital relationship. This process enables you to address the old, stale gender issues that plague our traditional notions of marriage. This is the path that brings you and your spouse together to challenge the social factors that otherwise would limit your ability to achieve an equitable relationship.

In this book, I have challenged the outdated idea that marriage should be organized around different and complementary roles for husbands and wives, i.e., the companionable breadwinner and homemaker. I am not the only person pushing for equitable marriages to flourish. This book, however, is unique in that it integrates the need to challenge gender as the appropriate motif for marriage with your willingness to be self-reflective and to work on managing your personal issues. I believe the two go together.

Sociologists have told us about the external social factors that limit couples' ability to achieve an equitable relationship. We know the work world has not yet adapted fully to the changing roles of men and women. We know that the lack of social support for such things as universal childcare and flexible work schedules continues to burden families seeking an equitable marriage. We have learned that men and women are finding it difficult to work things out in the face of such obstacles to their wishes for an equitable marriage.

Men and women are "settling" today in disastrously divergent ways. For men, this means they prefer to fall back on a neotraditional arrangement in which their paid work is their primary contribution to their marriage and family, and they expect their wife to take on the major share of household chores and childcare. Women, in contrast, are settling for something entirely different: having decided that being self-reliant is better than being economically dependent on a marriage that might not last, they are opting out of marriage altogether. These outcomes are not good for individual people, they are not good for marriage, they are not good for our economy, and they are not good for our society.

The ongoing process of collaborative negotiation between self-reflective, equally valued partners supports both individual partners *and* marriage relationships. Couples in marriages that have been created through this method are in a good position to address the limitations society tries to put on their equitable relationship. In doing this, you can shape the society in which you live for the betterment of everyone. The path is difficult—but the effort is worth it. I hope the guidelines I've set forth here for how to achieve a satisfying, loving, enjoyable, challenging, exciting, and equitable marriage will make the way easier for you.

APPENDIX A

The Unfinished Revolution

The Unfinished Revolution is the report of an extensive ethnographic research project conducted by Kathleen Gerson. Dr. Gerson, who is a tenured professor at New York University, is an authority on gender equality (particularly within relationships and marriages), changing gender roles, family housework patterns, and other aspects of changing family life. Dr. Gerson was interested in hearing from young people about growing up in a time of much upheaval in families, with women entering the workplace in significant numbers, divorce rates increasing, people cohabiting instead of marrying, and the era of the single-male-wage-earner just having ended. She wanted to know how these turbulent times of change affected the way young people thought about marriage, work, and family. Here is a brief review of her findings:

The People

Dr. Gerson interviewed 120 randomly chosen men and women between the ages of eighteen and thirty-two, with an average age of twenty-four at the time of the interviews.

An equal number of men and women with a broad range of racial, ethnic, and class backgrounds (55 percent non-Hispanic white, 22 percent African-American, 17 percent Latino/a, and 6 percent Asian) participated.

Regarding class, 46 percent of participants had a middle-class or upper-class background; 38 percent were from a working-class background; and 16 percent lived in or on the edge of poverty.

Format of the Study

In-depth interviews were conducted with each participant's life history, with each individual:

+ Describing their experiences growing up
+ Reflecting on the significance of these growing-up experiences
+ Sharing their hopes and plans for the future

Findings from the Study

Gerson's interviews showed a big gap between what young people's ideals about family life were and what the choices they felt they actually had were, primarily due to inflexible workplaces and lack of good support for childcare. One respondent put it this way: "Sometimes I ask myself if it's unrealistic to want everything. I think a lot of people will settle for something that is not what they wished."

Reported Experiences of Family Life

Here are the major findings about how these young people experienced their varied family lives:

+ The majority expressed strong support for working mothers. Half of young people thought mothers who did not have sustained work wished they had.

+ Four out of five participants who had work-committed mothers thought this was the best option.

+ The majority of participants expressed greater concern for the quality of their parents' relationship than whether they stayed together or not.

+ A slight majority of those who'd grown up in a single-parent home wished their biological parents had stayed together.

+ Almost half of participants believed it was better, if not ideal, for parents to separate than live in conflict-ridden or silent, unhappy homes.

+ Most young people from intact homes think staying intact was best, while two out of five felt their parents might have been better off splitting up.

Perceived Options

The reason for the title *The Unfinished Revolution* is that the young people Gerson interviewed were opting for second-best options, and these options are quite different for men and women.

For women:

+ Most of the women in the study emphasized self-reliance over economic dependence on a relationship that might not last.

+ Not marrying requires the double task of work and home responsibilities.

For men:

+ The men in the study opted for a return to a neotraditional arrangement.

+ Paid work is seen as their primary contribution to the marriage and family.

+ Though they are willing to help out at home, they expect their wife to take on a larger share of household labor.

Gerson emphasizes that these divergent fallback positions will perpetuate gender inequalities, regardless of these young people's desire to maintain gender and economic equality. As she notes, "In an era of economic and marital uncertainty, social supports for flexible, egalitarian blends of work and caretaking are essential to helping new generations care for their children and realize their own dreams. The answer to twenty-first-century conundrums is to finish the gender revolution, not turn back the clock."

APPENDIX B

Important Marital Issues to Negotiate

Being intentional, deliberate, and purposeful about your marriage means being willing to negotiate collaboratively around the issues you will face together over the course of your marriage.

How to Talk to Your Spouse

You start a conversation knowing your own thoughts and feelings about a topic. Remember, you want an opportunity to discuss these thoughts and feelings; your partner also wants the same opportunity. Here are some tips:

+ In your conversation, stick to your own thoughts and feelings. Don't get sidetracked by accusing, criticizing, or blaming your partner.

+ Be prepared to talk about what you want in a clear and direct fashion. Be cautious about lapsing into "I need" as a way of privileging what you want over your partner's wants. For example, say, "I would like more affection from you" rather than, "I need you to be more affectionate with me."

+ What you want in your relationship may reflect old issues from your personal history. Be sure to continually "vet" your wants and wishes.

+ Be willing to own up to where these wants come from; be willing to talk about painful personal histories, unfulfilled childhood needs, and the way you protect yourself from these old, painful childhood experiences.

+ Be sure to treat your partner with the respect and decency with which you treat any other person.

How to Listen to Your Spouse

Listen to your spouse with an unconditional interest in understanding what he/she is trying to say. This is the way to get to know your spouse and what it is important to him/her. Here are a few thoughts about listening:

+ Listening isn't about you; it's about your spouse, who really wants to be heard.

+ Be sure to focus on what your spouse is saying, not your reaction to it. If you find yourself reacting, take a time-out to refocus on your spouse.

+ It will be helpful to indicate that you are listening to your spouse while they're speaking. You can try reflecting what you are hearing him/her say so he/she can correct you if you are not understanding what is being said. For example, you can say, "I hear you say _____; is that right?"

+ By listening intently to your partner, you may learn something new about her/him and about the ideas and feelings she/he has. You can gain a new perspective about your partner.

Important Conversations to Have with Your Spouse

The format I've used in the following pages for discussing and negotiating goals as a couple comes from a booklet called "The Commitment Conversation," published by The Equality in Marriage Institute (the booklet is no longer in print). The Equality in Marriage Institute was founded by Lorna Jorgenson Wendt, who was an American corporate wife whose challenge to the divorce laws in Connecticut set a precedent for valuing the economic worth of corporate spouses. She argued that a wife is a 50-50 partner in a marriage, and therefore worth half of the assets. She was eventually awarded about one-fifth of the estimated worth of her and her husband's estate after her high-profile divorce put her in the international media spotlight. Lorna, fighting for equality in marriage, was willing to go public with a very private matter—and in doing so, she started a national discussion on fairness and equality in marriage and divorce. Dedicated to helping others understand and obtain equality before, during, and after marriage, Wendt founded the Equality in Marriage Institute. The institute is no longer active, but "The Commitment Conversation" is full of valuable questions and suggestions for married couples.

INDIVIDUAL AND JOINT GOALS

Here are three questions you can use to facilitate your discussion about goals:

1. What do you want as individuals in the future (one, five, and ten years from now)? What about careers, children, where to live, ideal futures?

2. How will you achieve these individual goals and remain a strong couple? Try creating a rough draft of how you can accomplish these goals together.

3. How can you help each other reach your goals?

LIFESTYLE

Here are items for discussing ideas and thoughts about the kind of lifestyle you want together:

1. Where will we live? What kind of home do we want? What about in the future?

2. How will you make time for each other? It is important to carve out time for each other.

FINANCES

Finances are difficult to talk about. Work to establish a plan for managing finances and a way to have ongoing conversations about your financial well-being as a couple:

1. What are your spending and saving habits?

2. Do you have separate assets and debts? Recognize that getting/being married makes your individual assets/debts joint assets/debts. Work to create a plan for spending and saving money.

3. Regularly discuss your financial goals and milestones.

4. Even as you manage your finances jointly, maintain your own financial and credit standing, perhaps by having separate checking accounts.

CHILDREN

Having and raising children is an intentional activity (as we discussed in depth in Chapter 9). Before having children, discuss and plan how you will work together to be effective parents, maintain gender equity, and sustain your relationship. Here are a few questions to talk to each other about:

1. Do you want children?

2. What are your parenting philosophies?

3. What is your plan for having and raising your children?

4. How will you go about sharing the responsibility of caring for your children?

HEALTH AND WELLNESS

Maintaining your individual health and wellness is part of a commitment to each other and your marriage.

1. How will you both maintain your physical health (e.g., nutrition, physical fitness, and individual health issues)?

2. How will you be supportive of each other's wishes to maintain physical health?

3. How will you each take care of your emotional and spiritual well-being?

SEXUALITY

Sexual intimacy is a vital part of your marital relationship. Be willing to talk openly with each other about sexual intimacy. (See Chapter 5 for how to talk openly with each other.)

LEGAL ISSUES

Besides being about love, friendship, and connection, marriage is also a legal union. Use the things you learn about having a good interpersonal relationship from this book to help you openly discuss important legal issues.

1. How will individual debts be managed in the marriage?

2. How will debt accrued in the marriage be handled?

3. If circumstances change, how will you divide marital assets?

4. How will you decide what health and life insurance plans to use?

5. How will you decide upon the beneficiaries of saving plans?

6. Should circumstances change, who will receive maintenance and/or child support from the other?

7. Create wills.

8. Are there individual premarital assets? Are these to remain with the individual?

Discussing and negotiating around these important areas of your marriage can enhance your marital relationship, so long as you utilize the tools and techniques of collaborative negotiation.

APPENDIX C

———

"Taking Things Personally Worksheet"

On the last page of this appendix, you will find the "Taking Things Personally Worksheet," which will help you understand when you are taking things personally and what your reaction is about. It is designed to help you learn to be more self-aware and therefore more proactive in your interactions with your spouse. You can make copies of this worksheet to try it out on events that occur in your relationship. Here are the steps to take to fill it out:

1. Pick out an incident that occurred recently between you and your spouse that caused some difficulty between the two of you. You may want to write down the incident as you recall it. I have used the interaction described in the text between Sara and Lucas as an example of how to complete this step:

   Sara and Lucas are in the living room together when she starts to tell him about an incident that happened to her at work. Lucas does not respond to her or engage with her around her comments. She angrily says to him, "How can you ignore me like that? I work so hard at being nice to you." Lucas looks up and says, "I don't know what you're talking about."

The worksheet, which is a personal inventory, is designed to sort out what is going on before this incident flairs into a nasty conflict. Let's take Sara's position, since she began the verbal interaction. Sara starts by sorting out her understanding of the episode by completing Columns 2, 3, and 4—"How Did I Experience the Event," "What Did I Feel," and "What Did I Do"—as follows: in Column 2, "Lucas was being inconsiderate to me"; in Column 3, "I was very angry and hurt at the same time"; and in Column 4, "I angrily accused Lucas of ignoring me and asked how he could do that to me.

You are to fill in the columns in the same way—sharing what you experienced, how you felt, and what you did. Be as clear as you can in telling what you experienced and what you did. Filling out these three columns requires you to identify your "part" in the negative interaction with your spouse. It is the beginning step in reflecting on how you experienced the situation and how you reacted to it.

2. Now is the time for reflection on your experience of the situation. Let's look at what Lucas did in the interaction with Sara. He did not pay attention to Sara in a way that she expected and wanted him to. This **description** of what Lucas did goes in Column 1, "Describing My Spouse's Action." By comparing Column 1 with Column 2, you can see the difference between describing something that happened and interpreting it as being about you. It is the difference between Sara accusing Lucas of **ignoring** her and her saying, "You did not pay attention the way I wanted you to." The first response will put Lucas on the defensive; the second opens the opportunity for discussion.

Further self-reflection is needed to understand how this experience of feeling ignored is threatening to Sara. Feeling ignored suggests that Sara thinks Lucas is not interested enough in her to pay attention, she is not a priority for him, he isn't enthusiastic about being with her, she is feeling discounted, etc. These are the fearful thoughts that are behind the accusation of being ignored that are the personal **threats** to Sara.

Now you must take the time to reflect on what way you are feeling threatened in the situation you are working on to fill in the final column, Column 5—"What is the Threat to Me." One tool you can use to help discover the threat is the Downward Arrow Technique I introduced in Chapter 3. Here is an example of how the Downward Arrow would work in Sara's situation.

How Sara Used the Downward Arrow Technique

In the example, Sara felt that Lucas was ignoring her. Sara would begin by asking herself a series of questions about Lucas ignoring her as follows:

Question	Answer
What does this mean about me?	It means Lucas doesn't care about me.
What does this (Lucas doesn't care) to mean about me?	It means he really isn't a good husband to me.
What does this (Lucas isn't good to me) mean about me?	It means I don't have a husband who cares and respects me.
What does this (Lucas doesn't) respect me) mean about me?	It must mean there is something wrong with me because he doesn't care about and respect me.
	If Lucas doesn't care about and respect me, maybe I am not worth caring about.

Threat: I am not worth caring about

Once your self-reflection process has provided you with perspective on the situation, you can assess what the problem is (or is not). For example, if Lucas typically does pay attention, once Sara has worked through her immediate reaction, she may not even perceive the lack of attentiveness in this situation as a problem. However, if lack of attentiveness is more typical of Lucas's actions toward Sara, she will want to address this with him using the methods of addressing issues we went over in Chapter 2.

Working on the difference between describing an event and how you experienced it (the distinction between the first two columns on the worksheet) is the difference between identifying problems you can work on with your spouse and reacting to him/her in an accusing fashion, which often leads to conflict. If you make the effort, you can get good at this. Good interpersonal interactions between you and your spouse require you to have the skill to make this kind of distinction.

Taking Things Personally Inventory

Column 1	Column 2	Column 3	Column 4	Column 5
Describe the event.	How did I experience the event?	What did I feel?	What did I do?	What is threat to me?
(Lucas did not pay attention to Sara when she was talking.)	(Lucas was being inconsiderate to me. He was ignoring me.)	(I was so angry and hurt at the same time.)	(I angrily accused him of ignoring me. How could he do that to me?)	(*As an adult*: I am not important to him. *As a child*: I am not an important person worthy of attention.)

APPENDIX D

Articles on Living with a Mentally Ill Spouse

Alcoholism: "Guide to Living with an Alcoholic," DualDiagnosis.org: http://www.dualdiagnosis.org/alcohol-addiction/guide-living-alcoholic.

Asperger's. "Dealing with an Asperger's Husband: Tips for Married Couples," Chat for Adults with HFA and Asperger's: http://www.adultaspergerschat.com/2012/04/dealing-with-aspergers-husband-tips-for.html.

Bipolar Disorder. Sue Sanders and Francesca Castagnoli, "I Lost My Husband to Bipolar Disorder": http://www.cnn.com/2013/07/24/health/change-mind-real-simple.

Borderline Personality Disorder (BPD): Linda Spadin, "Living with and Loving Someone with Borderline Personality Disorder," PsychCentral: http://psychcentral.com/blog/archives/2013/11/15/living-with-loving-someone-with-borderline-personality-disorder.

Depression. Sari Harrar, "How to Deal with a Depressed Spouse": http://www.rd.com/health/wellness/how-to-cope-with-a-depressed-spouse.

Narcissism. Craig Maskin. "7 Strategies for Dealing with the Narcissist You Love." *Huffington Post*: http://www.huffingtonpost.com/dr-craig-malkin/7-strategies-for-dealing-_b_5192851.html.

Paranoid. Carrie Barron, "7 Tips for Coping with a Paranoid Partner," *Psychology Today*: https://www.psychologytoday.com/blog/the-creativity-cure/201601/7-tips-coping-paranoid-partner.

Psychosis. Mark Lukach, "My Lovely Wife in the Psych Ward," *The Pacific Standard*: https://psmag.com/my-lovely-wife-in-the-psych-ward-2edac99d046e#.ptfh2zxx9 *(This is a truly remarkable story about a husband's love for his ill wife.)*

PTSD (Post-Traumatic Stress Disorder) and TBI (Traumatic Brain Injury): "To the Spouses Who Are Enduring Hell," *Living with PTSD and TBI*: http://armyreservistwife.blogspot.com/2010/06/to-spouses-who-are-enduring-hell.html.

ENDNOTES

INTRODUCTION

1. Kathleen Gerson, *The Unfinished Revolution: Coming of Age in a New Era of Gender, Work, and Family* (New York: Oxford University Press, 2011), 10–12.

CHAPTER 1:
A NEW PERSPECTIVE

1. Sarah Fenstermaker Berk, *The Gender Factor: The Apportionment of Work in American Households* (New York: Plenum Press, 1985), 201–208. Berk studied the links between gender and household work describing the home as a small factory, one in which the prime mover of how tasks were allocated was by gender, i.e., "They 'do' gender as they 'do' housework and childcare, and what I have been calling the division of household labor provides for the joint production of household labor and gender . . ."

2. Christopher Coulson, "What is Collaboration?" *Dynamic Living™* (blog), October 2003, http://www.santafecoach.com/dl/oct03.htm#parting.

CHAPTER 2:
THE NEGOTIATION PROCESS

1. Philip Kitcher, *Science, Truth, and Democracy* (New York: Oxford University Press, 2003), 117–118. I try to be very precise in the language I use. One of my pet peeves is the way in which people in my profession do not differentiate between a disagreement and a conflict. These are significantly different things in a relationship or marriage.

2. Lisa F. Barrett, "What Emotions Are (And Aren't)," *New York Times*, July 23, 2015, Sunday Review.

3. Jennifer Porter, "Why You Should Make Time for Self-Reflection (Even If You Hate Doing It)." *Harvard Business Review* (March 21, 2017), https://hbr.org/2017/03/why-you-should-make-time-for-self-reflection-even-if-you-hate-doing-it.

4. Daniel Goleman, *Emotional Intelligence* (New York: Bantam Books, 1995), 16–24.

5. David Viscott, *The Language of Feelings* (Priam Books, 1976), 35, 51, and 75.

6. Margarita Tartakovsky, "How Conflict Can Improve Your Relationship," *PsychCentral Blog*, 2016, https://psychcentral.com/ib/how-conflict-can-improve-your-relationship/. The disagreement described between Sara and Lucas was adapted from this post. Of course, I disagree with the use of the concept of conflict to describe the couple's disagreement, but it is a useful example of a problem that was solved through negotiation, which is the point.

CHAPTER 3:
TAKING CARE OF YOUR PERSONAL ISSUES

1. Jay Spence, "The Downward Arrow Technique (If You Lose Your Pen, You Will Die)," *Jay Spence Blog*, July 20, 2012, http://jayspence.blogspot.com/2012/07/the-downward-arrow-technique-if-you.html.

2. Shauna Mackenzie, "Overcome My Insecurities? No Thank You," *Best Kept Self Blog*, http://www.bestkeptself.com/overcome-insecurities-thank.

CHAPTER 4:
WHERE DO INSECURITIES COME FROM?

1. Gershen Kaufman, *Shame: The Power of Caring* (Rochester, Vermont: Schenkman Books, Inc., 1985), 40–41.

CHAPTER 5:
ENJOYING SEX

1. Esther Perel, *Mating in Captivity: Unlocking Erotic Intelligence* (New York: Harper, 2007), 25–27. Perel's work is excellent and will be helpful to couples who want to maintain a vibrant sexual relationship throughout their marriage.

2. Perel, 17–18.

3. Perel, 10–12.

4. Perel, 47–51

5. Perel, 97–100

6. Perel, 107–108

7. Perel, 108–109

8. Terri D. Conley et al., "Methodological and Conceptual Insights That Narrow, Reframe, and Eliminate Gender Differences in Sexuality," *Current Directions in Psychological Science* 20, no. 5 (2011): 296–300. Terri Conley is a professor of psychology at the University of Michigan who does research on the myths about women's sexuality. You can read about her and her research in a February 14, 2014, article in *New York Magazine* (http://nymag.com/thecut/2014/02/woman-with-an-alternative-theory-of-hookups.html) titled, "Meet Terri Conley: The Psychologist With an Alternative Theory of Hookup Culture" by Kat Stoeffel. Here is what Dr. Conley says about herself in this article: "Being

willing to think about things from a non-dominant perspective is a legacy of my association with women's studies. I was lying awake in bed a few weeks ago thinking about why my papers get rejected more than most people's and it occurred to me that every single paper I wrote has someone it's trying to take down or someone I'm mad at. I have sort of an adversarial approach to science, which I actually think is very healthy for science."

9. Lori Gottlieb, "Does a More Equal Marriage Mean Less Sex," *New York Times Magazine*, February 6, 2014. This article got a lot of press, as you might imagine. Here are a few of the headlines generated by this article from a 2013 post by *LibbyAnne* (http://www.patheos.com/blogs/lovejoyfeminism/2013/01/more-chores-for-men-less-sex.html) that will give you good examples of how the press can distort research findings about gender and sex (in particular):

- "It may be the 21st century, but a new study suggests sticking to old values may reap benefit—that is, if you like sex."

- "Want to have more sex? Men, stop helping with the chores."

- "Why husbands who share household chores miss out on sex"

10. Dan Carlson et al., "The Gendered Division of Housework and Couples' Sexual Relationships: A Re-Examination," (2014), https://scholarworks.gsu.edu/cgi/viewcontent.cgi?article=1002&context=sociology_facpub.

11. Hal Arkowitz and Scott O. Lilienfeld, "Sex in Bits and Bytes: What's the Problem?" *Scientific American Mind*, July 1, 2010, http://www.scientificamerican.com/article/sex-in-bits-and-bytes/.

12. Davy Rothbart, "He's Just Not That into Anyone: Even, and Perhaps Especially, When His Girlfriend Is Acting Like the Women He Can't Stop Watching Online," *New York Magazine*, January 30, 2011, http://nymag.com/news/features/70976/.

13. David Rosen, "Is the Rise of Filthy Gonzo Porn Actually Dangerous, Or Are People Overreacting?" *Alternet*, June 7, 2013, https://www.alternet.org/sex-amp-relationships/gonzo-porn.

CHAPTER 6:
THE UNEXAMINED MALE LIBIDO

1. Stephen Marche, "The Unexamined Brutality of the Male Libido," *New York Times*, November 25, 2017, Sunday Review, https://www.-nytimes.com/2017/11/25/opinion/sunday/harassment-men-libido-masculinity.html. Marche wrote "The Unmade Bed," which describes his experience in moving to Canada because his wife got a great job there. His wife has a running commentary in the book, very innovative.

2. Richard Reeves and Isabel Sawhill, "Men's Lib!" *New York Times*, November 14, 2015, Sunday Review, https://www.nytimes.com/2015/11/15/opinion/sunday/mens-lib.html.

3. Susan Faludi, *Stiffed: The Betrayal of the American Man* (New York: William Morrow Paperbacks, 2000), 38–39.

4. Marche, *The Unexamined Brutality*.

5. Andrew Romano, "Why We Need to Reimagine Masculinity," *Newsweek*, September 20, 2010, http://www.newsweek.com/why-we-need-reimagine-masculinity-71993.

6. Romano, "Reimagine Masculinity."

7. Sari Van Anders, "Testosterone and Sexual Desire in Healthy Women and Men," *Archives of Sexual Behavior* 41, no. 6 (2012): 1471–84.

CHAPTER 7:
CHOOSING FIDELITY

1. *Statistic Brain,* "Infidelity Statistics," https://www.statisticbrain.com/infidelity-statistics/.

2. Peggy Vaughan, *The Monogamy Myth: A Personal Handbook for Recovering from Affairs* (New York: William Morrow Paperbacks, 2003), 30–40.

3. Perel, *Mating in Captivity,* 176–178.

4. Tammy Nelson, "How the 'New Monogamy' is Keeping Relationships Together," *Alternet,* February 17, 2015, https://www.alternet.org/sex-amp-relationships/how-new-monogamy-keeping-relationships-together.

5. Nelson, "New Monogamy."

CHAPTER 8:
BALANCING FAMILY AND WORK

1. Susan Pease Gadoua and Vicki Larson, *The New "I Do"* (Berkeley, California: Seal Press, 2014).

2. Richard Reeves, "How to Save Marriages in America," *The Atlantic,* February 13, 2014, https://www.theatlantic.com/business/archive/2014/02/how-to-save-marriage-in-america/283732/. This is a good article about marriage. He has an entertaining chart about the three kinds of marriages he describes.

3. R. J. Ely et al., "Rethink What You 'Know' About High-Achieving Women," *Harvard Business Review,* December 2014, https://hbr.org/2014/12/rethink-what-you-know-about-high-achieving-women.

4. Linda Thompson, "Conceptualizing Gender in Marriage: The Case of Marital Care," *Journal of Marriage and Family* 55, no. 3 (1993): 564–65.

5. Noah Berlatsky, "Spouses Probably Shouldn't Try to Split Household Tasks Exactly Evenly." *The Atlantic*, March 19, 2013. This is an excellent article, a bit theoretical about debt in relationship to managing household chores, but worth the effort.

6. Stephen Marche, "The Case for Filth," *New York Times*, December 12, 2013, Sunday Review, http://www.nytimes.com/2013/12/08/opinion/sunday/the-case-for-filth.html.

7. Jeff Grabmeier, "When the Baby Comes, Working Couples No Longer Share Housework Equally," The Ohio State University New Parents Project, *The Ohio State University*, https://news.osu.edu/news/2015/05/07/new baby/. This is a longitudinal study about status of egalitarian marriages. Having a baby propels you to a more gendered arrangement if you are not careful.

8. Shelley Haddock et al., "Ten Adaptive Strategies for Family and Work Balance: Advice from Successful Couples." *Journal of Marital and Family Therapy* 27, no. 4 (2001): 445–58.

9. Jena McGregor, "How Do You Erase the Taboo of Paternity Leave?" *The Washington Post*, June 18, 2015, https://www.washingtonpost.com/news/on-leadership/wp/2015/06/18/companies-try-to-erase-the-taboo-of-paternity-leave/.

10. Edwards, Kasey. "How Men Can Fight for Workplace Flexibility." *Fatherly*, June 12, 2017. www.smh.com.au/lifestyle/life-and-relationships/heres-how-men-can-fight-for-workplace-flexibility-if-they-really-want-it-20170611-gwp0q4.html.

CHAPTER 9:
SHARING PARENTING

1. Jennifer Senior, "All Joy and No Fun: The Paradox of Modern Parenting," *New York Magazine*, July 4, 2010, https://www.google. com/searchq=jennifer+senior+all+joy+and+no+fun+new+york +magazine+2010&oq=Jen&aqs=chrome1.69i57j69i59l3j0l2.5025j0j 8&sourceid=chrome&ie=UTF-8.

2. Matthew White and Paul Dolan, "Accounting for the Richness of Daily Activities," *Psychological Science* 20 (2009): 1000–08.

3. Christine Overall, *Why Have Children? The Ethical Debate* (Cambridge, MA: MIT Press, 2009).

4. Senior, "All Joy and No Fun."

5. Lisa Belkin, "When Mom and Dad Share It All," *The New York Times Magazine*, June 15, 2008, http://www.nytimes.com/ 2008/06/15/magazine/15parenting-t.html.

6. Nicholas Townsend, *The Package Deal: Marriage, Work, and Fatherhood in Men's Lives* (Philadelphia, PA: Temple University Press, 2002), 2–3.

7. Anne Storey and Katherine Wynne-Edwards, "Hormonal Correlates of Paternal Responsiveness in New and Expectant Fathers," *Evolution and Human Behavior* 21, no. 2 (2000) 79–95.

8. Peter B. Gray et al., "Testosterone and Marriage among Ariaal Men of Northern Kenya," *Current Anthropology* 48, no. 5 (2007): 750–55.

9. Peter B. Gray et al., "Hormonal Correlates of Human Paternal Interactions: A Hospital-Based Investigation In Urban Jamaica," *Hormones and Behavior* 52, no. 4 (2007): 499–507.

10. Yevgenia Kozorovitskiy et al., "Fatherhood Affects Dendritic Spines and Vasopressin V1a Receptors in the Primate Prefrontal Cortex," *Nature Neuroscience* 9 (2006): 1094–95.

11. Steve Almond, "Bimbo Proof the Nursery," *Best Life* (December 2007/January 2008): 106–08.

12. Judith Warner, *Perfect Madness: Motherhood in the Age of Anxiety* (New York: Riverhead Books, 2006).

13. Stephanie Coontz, "The Family in Upheaval." *Stephanie Coontz.com*, June 19, 2005, http://www.stephaniecoontz.com/ articles/article17.htm.

14. Nancy Heath, "How to Evaluate Parenting Resources," *She Knows*, June 17, 2014, http://www.sheknows.com/community/ parenting/how-to-evaluate-parenting-resources.

15. Gail Goss, "Why More Women Choose Not to Have Children," *HUFFPOST Blog*, posted September 25, 2016, https:// www.huffingtonpost.com/dr-gail-gross/why-more-women-choosenot-to-have-children_b_8039694.html.

16. Elizabeth Plank, "The Truth About Women Who Don't Have Kids," MIC, April 29, 2015, https://mic.com/articles/116676/ what-s-wrong-with-women-who-don-t-want-kids#.qKnwmTaxY.

17. Moira Weigel, "The Foul Reign of the Biological Clock," *The Guardian*, May 10, 2016.

CHAPTER 10:
GENDER TRAPS

1. Ely, "Rethink What You 'Know.'"

2. Alice Freed, "We Understand Perfectly: A Critique of Tannen's View of Cross-sex Communication." In *Locating Power: Proceedings of The Second Berkeley Women and Language Conference* (vol. 1), eds.

Kira Hall, et al. Berkeley: Berkeley Women and Language Group (1992), 144–152, https://www.montclair.edu/media/montclairedu/chss/departments/linguistics/Tannen-Review-Berk92.pdf.

3. Louann Brizendine, *The Female Brain* (New York City: Harmony, 2006).

4. Mark Liberman, "The Main Job of the Girl Brain," *Language Log* (blog), August 6, 2006, http://itre.cis.upenn.edu/~myl/languagelog/archives/003530.html.

5. Deborah James and Janice Drakich, "Understanding Gender Differences in Amount of Talk: Critical Review of Research," In *Gender and Conversational Interaction*, ed. Deborah Tannen (New York: Oxford University Press, 1993).

6. Bobbi Carothers and Harry Reis, "Men and Women Are from Earth: Examining the Latent Structure of Gender," *Journal of Personality and Social Psychology* 104, no. 2 (2013).

7. Eric Sentell, "Why Sacrificing Power Helps Husbands Gain Masculinity," *Role Reboot: Life Off Script* (blog), September 13, 2011, http://www.rolereboot.org/culture-and-politics/details/2011-09-why-sacrificing-power-helps-husbands-gain-masculinit.

8. Russell B. Lemle, "How Being Entitled to Our Way—Gets in the Way," *Psychology Today* (blog), August 21, 2011, https://www.psychologytoday.com/blog/me-first-we-first/20108/how-being-entitled-our-way-gets-in-the-way.

9. John M. Gottman and Nan Silver, "Principle 4: Let Your Partner Influence You," *The Seven Principles for Making Marriages Work* (New York: Crown Publishers, Inc., 1999), 99–102.

10. K.A. Eldridge and A. Christensen, "Demand-Withdraw Communication During Couple Conflict: A Review and Analysis," In *Understanding Marriage: Developments in the Study of Couple Interaction*, eds. P. Noller and J.A. Feeney (New York: Cambridge University Press, 2002).

11. Gottman and Silver, 27–34.

12. Barry Deutsch, "The Male Privilege Checklist: An Unabashed Imitation of an Article by Peggy McIntosh," https://www.cpt.org/files/US%20-%20Male%20Privilege%20Checklist.pdf.

13. Stephanie Ellen Byrd. "Life Happens: Understanding Specialization and Adaptation of Women Transitioning between Traditional and Dual-Career Families." (2006). Annual Meeting of the *American Sociological Association* Meeting, Montreal"

14. Ely, "Rethink What You 'Know.'"

CHAPTER 11:
WHEN YOUR SPOUSE IS MENTALLY ILL

1.Sandy Malone, "Mental Health in Marriage," *HUFFPOST Blog*, November 23, 2012, http://ww.huffingtonpost.com/sandy-malone/mental-health-in-a-mar1904140.html. riage_b_1904140.html.

2. Mandy Walker, "Deciding to Divorce When Your Spouse Has a Mental Illness," *Since My Divorce Blog*, February 19, 2014, http://sincemydivorce.com/about-me.

BIBLIOGRAPHY

Almond, Steve. "Bimbo Proof the Nursery." *Best Life*, December 2007/January 2008.

Arkowitz, Hal and Scott O. Lilienfeld. "Sex in Bits and Bytes: What's the Problem? How Destructive Is Internet Porn?" *Scientific American Mind*, 2010. http://www.scientificamerican.com/article/sex-in-bits-and-bytes/.

Barrett, L. F. "What Emotions Are (And Aren't)." *New York Times, Sunday*, January 17, 2016.

Belkin, Lisa. "When Mom and Dad Share It All." *The New York Times Magazine.* June 15, 2008. http://www.nytimes.com/2008/06/15/magazine/15parenting-t.html.

Berk, Sarah Fenstermaker. *The Gender Factor: The Apportionment of Work in American Households*. New York: Plenum, 1985.

Berlatsky, Noah. "Spouses Probably Shouldn't Try to Split Household Tasks Exactly Evenly." *The Atlantic*. March 19, 2013.

Best Kept Self Blog. http://www.bestkeptself.com/oversome-insecurities-thank/.

Brizidine, Louann. *The Female Brain*. New York: Harmony, 2006.

Carlson, Dan, Amanda J. Miller, Sharon Sassler, and Sarah Hanson. "The Gendered Division of Housework and Couples' Sexual Relationships: A Re-Examination." https://scholarworks.gsu.edu/cgi/viewcontent.cgi?article=1002&context=sociology_facpub.

Carothers, Bobbi and Harry Reis. "Men and Women Are from Earth: Examining the Latent Structure of Gender." *Journal of Personality and Social Psychology* 104, no. 2 (2013). Eub2012Oct22.

Conley, Terri D., Amy C. Moors, Jes L. Matsick, Ali Ziegler, & Brandon A. Valentine. "Methodological and Conceptual Insights That Narrow, Reframe, and Eliminate Gender Differences in Sexuality." *Current Directions in Psychological Science* 20, no. 5 (2011).

Coontz, Stephanie. "The Family in Upheaval." *Stephanie Coontz.com.* http://www.stephaniecoontzcom/articles/article17.htm.

Coulson, Christopher. "What is Collaboration?" *DynamicLiving*™. http://www.santafecoach.com/dl/oct03.htm#parting.

Deutsch, Barry. "The Male Privilege Checklist: An Unabashed Imitation of an Article by Peggy McIntosh." https://www.cpt.org/files/US%20-%20Male%20Privilege%20Checklist.pdf.

Douthat, Ross. "Is Pornography Adultery?" *The Atlantic.* October 2008.

Eldridge, K.A. and A. Christensen. "Demand-Withdraw Communication During Couple Conflict: A Review and Analysis." In P. Noller and J.A. Feeney (Eds.). *Understanding Marriage: Developments in the Study of Couple Interaction.* New York: Cambridge University Press, 2002.

Ely, Robin J., Pamela Stone, and Colleen Ammerman, "Rethink What You 'Know' About High-Achieving Women." *Harvard Business Review.* December 2014. https://hbr.org/2014/12/rethink-what-you-know-about-high-achieving-women.

Faludi, Susan. *Stiffed: The Betrayal of the American Man.* New York: William Morrow Paperbacks, 2000.

Freed, Alice. "We Understand Perfectly: A Critique of Tannen's View of Cross-sex Communication." In *Locating Power: Proceedings of The Second Berkeley Women and Language Conference* (vol. 1), eds. Kira Hall, Mary Bucholtz, and Birch Moonwomon Berkeley: Berkeley Women and Language Group, 1992.

Gadoua, Susan Pease and Vicki Larson. *The New "I Do."* Berkeley, California: Seal Press, 2014.

Gerson, Kathleen. *The Unfinished Revolution: Coming of Age in a New Era of Gender, Work and Family.* New York: Oxford University Press, 2011.

Goleman, Daniel. *Emotional Intelligence.* New York: Bantam Books, 1995.

Gottlieb, Lori. "Does a More Equal Marriage Mean Less Sex." *New York Times Magazine,* https://www.nytimes.com/2014/02/09/magazine/does-a-more-equal-marriage-mean-less-sex.html.

Gottman, John M. and Nan Silver. *The Seven Principles for Making Marriage Work.* New York: Crown Publishers, Inc., 1999.

Grabmeier, Jeff. "When the Baby Comes, Working Couples No Longer Share Housework Equally." The Ohio State University New Parents Project, *The Ohio State University.* https://news.osu.edu/news/2015/05/07/new-baby/.

Gray, Peter B., J.C. Parking, and M.E. Samms Vaughan. "Hormonal Correlates of Human Paternal Interactions: A Hospital-Based Investigation in Urban Jamaica." *Hormones and Behavior* 52, no. 5 (2007).

Gray, Peter B., Peter T. Ellison, and Benjamin C. Campbell. "Testosterone and Marriage among Ariaal Men of Northern Kenya." *Current Anthropology* 48, no. 5 (October 2007).

Haddock, Shelley A., Toni S. Zimmerman, Scott J. Ziemba, and Lisa R. Current. "Ten Adaptive Strategies for Family and Work Balance: Advice from Successful Couples." *Journal of Marital and Family Therapy* 27, no. 4 (October 2001): 445–458.

HuffPost Blog. https://www.huffingtonpost.com/dr-gail-gross/
why-more-women-choosenot-to-have-children_b_8039694.html.

HuffPost Blog. http://ww.huffingtonpost.com/sandy-malone/
mental-health-in-a-mar1904140.html. riage_b_1904140.html.

Israelsen-Hartley, Sara. "Millennials Plan to Trade Kids for Careers
—But It Doesn't Have to be That Way." *Deseret National News*.
March 16, 2014.

James, Deborah and Janice Drakich. "Understanding Gender
Differences in Amount of Talk: Critical Review of Research." In
Tannen, Deborah (ed.). *Gender and Conversational Interaction*. New
York: Oxford University Press, 1993.

Jay Spence Blog. http://jayspence.blogspot.com/2012/07/the-
downward-arrow-technique-if-you.html

Kaufman, Gershen. *Shame: The Power of Caring*. Rochester,
Vermont: Schenkman Books, Inc., 1985.

Kitcher, Philip. *Science, Truth, and Democracy*. New York: Oxford
University Press, 2003.

Kozorovitskiy, Yevgenia, Maria Hughes, Kim Lee, and Elizabeth
Gould. "Fatherhood Affects Dendritic Spines and Vasopressin V1a
Receptors in The Primate Prefrontal Cortex." *Nature Neuroscience* 9
(2006).

Language Log Blog. http://itre.cis.upenn.edu/~myl/languagelog/
archives/003530.html.

Marche, Stephen. "The Case for Filth." *New York Times*.
http://www.nytimes.com/2013/12/08/opinion/sunday/the-case-
for-filth.html.

Marche, Stephen. "The Unexamined Brutality of the Male Libido."
New York Times. https://www.nytimes.com/2017/11/25/opinion/
sunday/harassment-men-libido-masculinity.html.

McGregor, Jena. "How Do You Erase the Taboo of Paternity Leave?" *The Washington Post*. https://www.washingtonpost.com/news/on-leadership/wp/2015/06/18/companies-try-to-erase-the-taboo-of-paternity-leave/.

MIC Blog. https://mic.com/articles/116676/what-s-wrong-with-women-who-don-t-want-kids#.9lNq8KRa9.

Nelson, Tammy. "How the 'New Monogamy' is Keeping Relationships Together." *Alternet*. https://www.alternet.org/sex-amp-relationships/how-new-monogamy-keeping-relationships-together.

Overall, Christine. *Why Have Children? The Ethical Debate*. Cambridge: The MIT Press, 2009.

Perel, Esther. *Mating in Captivity: Unlocking Erotic Intelligence*. New York: Harper Paperbacks, 2007.

Porter, Jennifer. "Why You Should Make Time for Self-Reflection (Even If You Hate Doing It)." *Harvard Business Review*, March 21, 2017. https://hbr.org/2017/03/why-you-should-make-time-for-self-reflection-even-if-you-hate-doing-it.

Psychology Today Blog. https://www.psychologytoday.com/blog/me-first-we-first/20108/how-being-entitled-our-way-gets-in-the-way.

Reeves, Richard. "How to Save Marriages in America." *The Atlantic*. https://www.theatlantic.com/business/archive/2014/02/how-to-save-marriage-in-america/283732/.

Reeves, Richard and Isabel Sawhill. "Men's Lib!" *New York Times*. November 14, 2015, Sunday Review.

Romano, Andrew. "Why We Need to Reimagine Masculinity." *Newsweek*. http://www.newsweek.com/why-we-need-reimagine-masculinity-71993.

Rothbart, Davy. "He's Just Not That into Anyone: Even, and Perhaps Especially, When His Girlfriend is Acting Like the Women He Can't Stop Watching Online." *New York Magazine.* http://nymag.com/news/features/#print/.

Rosen, David. "Is the Rise of Filthy Gonzo Porn Actually Dangerous, Or Are People Overreacting?" *Alternet.* https://www.alternet.org/sex-amp-relationships/gonzo-porn.

She Knows Blog. http://www.sheknows.com/community/parenting/how-evaluate-parenting-resources.

Senior, Jennifer. "All Joy and No Fun: The Paradox of Modern Parenting." *New York Magazine.* July 4, 2010.

Since My Divorce Blog. http://sincemydivorce.com/about-me/ (accessed 10/22/17).

--- *Statistic Brain.* "Infidelity Statistics." https://www.statisticbrain.com/infidelity-statistics/.

Storey, Anne and Katherine Wynne-Edwards. "Hormonal Correlates of Paternal Responsiveness in New and Expectant Fathers." *Evolution and Human Behavior* 21, no. 2 (March 1, 2000).

Tartakovsky, Margarita. "*How Conflict Can Improve Your Relationship.*" https://psychcentral.com/lib/how-conflict-can-improve-your-relationship/.

Thompson, Linda. "Conceptualizing Gender in Marriage: The Case of Marital Care." *Journal of Marriage and Family* 55, no. 3 (August 1993).

Townsend, Nicholas. "Marriage, Work and Fatherhood in Men's Lives." Temple University Press, 2002.

Van Anders, Sari. "Testosterone and Sexual Desire in Healthy Women and Men." *Archives of Sexual Behavior* 41, no. 6 (2012).

Vaughan, Peggy. *The Monogamy Myth: A Personal Handbook for Recovering from Affairs*. New York: William Morrow Paperbacks, 2003.

Viscott, David. *The Language of Feelings*. (n.p.) Priam Books, 1976.

Warner, Judith. *Perfect Madness: Motherhood in the Age of Anxiety*. New York: Riverhead Books, 2006.

Weigel, Moira. "The Foul Reign of the Biological Clock." *The Guardian*. May 10, 2016.

West, Candace and Don Zimmerman. "Doing Gender." *Gender and Society* 1, no. 2 (1987).

White, Matthew, & Paul Dolan. "Accounting for The Richness of Daily Activities." *Psychological Science* 20 (2009).

Acknowledgments

This book is dedicated to my loving and equitable marriage partner, Dr. Joseph F. Aponte. It is further dedicated to my three terrific children, Chris, Ari, and Gabrielle. These are the people with whom I have shared most of my life; they all have contributed to my personal and professional well-being in a profound way. I love them and am grateful to them.

I also want to acknowledge the couples with whom I have worked professionally in my thirty-year career as a clinical psychologist. It is rewarding to be helpful to couples who are struggling in their relationships. Repairing relationships is hard work for everyone but worth the effort. My salute to all those with whom I have worked.

I sincerely appreciate the graduate students in the Clinical Psychology Program at Spalding University who dedicated their dissertations to testing both the theoretical and practical implications of my approach to working with couples.

A shout-out goes to Sheryl Connelly, the owner of Marketing Media Management. Sheryl was instrumental in helping me find my voice—first as a blog writer, then as an author—so I could effectively express my ideas about creating and maintaining an equitable and committed marriage. She has been a teacher, advisor, consultant, and friend.

My husband, Joe, has read and reread this manuscript, making many indispensable additions and corrections.

About the Author

CATHERINE APONTE is a clinical psychologist who is married to a clinical psychologist, Joseph F. Aponte. They married in 1960, a time of significant social change. She and her husband embarked upon a marital journey guided by the basic principle that neither one of their careers was more important than the other's. She trained as a psychologist at the University of Florida, Duke University, and Spalding University, and worked with couples for more than thirty years in Louisville, KY as a practicing psychologist. During her professional career both as a clinician in private practice and an adjunct professor of clinical psychology at Spalding University, she made numerous presentations about her work with couples. Both her master's thesis at Duke University and her doctoral thesis at Spalding University focused on gender and marriage. Aponte was awarded a USPHS Traineeship covering the four years she was a graduate student at Duke University, and had the privilege of chairing eight doctoral dissertations at Spalding University testing various aspects of her theoretical model of relationships.

SELECTED TITLES FROM SHE WRITES PRESS

She Writes Press is an independent publishing company
founded to serve women writers everywhere.
Visit us at www.shewritespress.com.

Note to Self: A Seven-Step Path to Gratitude and Growth by Laurie
Buchanan. $16.95, 978-1-63152-113-3. Transforming intention into
action, *Note to Self* equips you to shed your baggage, bridging the
gap between where you are and where you want to be—body, mind,
and spirit—and empowering you to step into joy-filled living *now!*

*The Thriver's Edge: Seven Keys to Transform the Way You Live, Love,
and Lead* by Donna Stoneham. $16.95, 978-1-63152-980-1. A
"coach in a book" from master executive coach and leadership expert Dr. Donna Stoneham, *The Thriver's Edge* outlines a practical
road map to breaking free of the barriers keeping you from being
everything you're capable of being.

*The Clarity Effect: How Being More Present Can Transform Your
Work and Life* by Sarah Harvey Yao. $16.95, 978-1-63152-958-0.
A practical, strategy-filled guide for stressed professionals looking
for clarity, strength, and joy in their work and home lives.

Think Better. Live Better. 5 Steps to Create the Life You Deserve by
Francine Huss. $16.95, 978-1-938314-66-7. With the help of this
guide, readers will learn to cultivate more creative thoughts, realign
their mindset, and gain a new perspective on life.

*The Way of the Mysterial Woman: Upgrading How You Live, Love,
and Lead* by Suzanne Anderson, MA and Susan Cannon, PhD.
$24.95, 978-1-63152-081-5. A revolutionary yet practical road
map for upgrading your life, work, and relationships that reveals
how your choice to transform is part of an astonishing future trend.

*Letting Go into Perfect Love: Discovering the Extraordinary After
Abuse* by Gwendolyn M. Plano. $16.95, 978-1-938314-74-2. After
staying in an abusive marriage for twenty-five years, Gwen Plano
finally broke free—and started down the long road toward healing.